AN ARTIST'S NOTES ON
HUMANS
AND THE
UNIVERSE

The World's Fundamental Laws of Nature:
Flux, Limitations, and the
Inborn Mechanism of Human Perceptions

V. NOVA

Archway Publishing books may be ordered through booksellers or by contacting:

Archway Publishing
1663 Liberty Drive
Bloomington, IN 47403
www.archwaypublishing.com
844-669-3957

Because of the dynamic nature of the Internet, any web addresses or links contained in this book may have changed since publication and may no longer be valid. The views expressed in this work are solely those of the author and do not necessarily reflect the views of the publisher, and the publisher hereby disclaims any responsibility for them.

Any people depicted in stock imagery provided by Getty Images are models, and such images are being used for illustrative purposes only.
Certain stock imagery © Getty Images.

ISBN: 978-1-6657-5701-0 (sc)
ISBN: 978-1-6657-5703-4 (hc)
ISBN: 978-1-6657-5702-7 (e)

Library of Congress Control Number: 2024903582

Print information available on the last page.

Archway Publishing rev. date: 08/28/2024

ACKNOWLEDGEMENTS

I would like to express my deep gratitude to the individuals who mercilessly humiliated me while writing this book without bothering to read it. I especially thank the people close to me who intentionally blamed me for "not working and thinking like a normal person." I thank those who have distracted me in many ways, causing me illness and grave depression. Eventually, I had to overcome my wretched obstacles and finish this first presentation of my unorthodox book, a lifelong journey into the deeply intuitive field of the mind, which I invite curious readers to personally discover within themselves.

If this writing somehow gains broader notice, I will not be surprised to face conventional criticism and its notorious host, a recycled-through-the-ages and profoundly confused archaic human psyche.

CONTENTS

INTRODUCTION

The Universal Laws of *Flux* and Its Unavoidable Limitations

There are no stars out there, no trees or water.

The world we are made of is a *Flux* that exists for less than an instant, entirely new, with all its births and deaths. **At its deep core, every living being keeps interacting with invisible instances of ever-changing conditions of nature. Nature is unstoppable change.** If the worlds of all existences are about instant transformations and therefore entirely metamorphic in their deepest stage, *how* can not just we but any sort of living being survive in this endless whirlpool of ever-new, unrepeatable nature?

Although our human bodily sensory organs are still poorly developed and no technologies can even remotely compensate for our physical inability to survive and evolve wisely, our pride and sense of superiority over other forms of existence only boldly reveal our weaknesses and unnecessary struggles compared to other forms of self-evolving life using neither artificial gadgets nor energies.

If we grasp the following further on in these writing observations, we could discover and possibly comprehend the precious gifts of nature that we human beings unintentionally bury behind the visible spectacles of the superficial consciousness of our playful minds, where they remain unnoticed to this day.

We still remain unaware of the endless instances of change that affect our entire existence as the deepest driving force of life.

What abilities are we as living beings granted by nature just to *be*? For the first time, we are about to recognize and describe this quintessential gift granted to us from birth as **nature's mechanism of perception**.

Our *perceiving* is a *process* revealing our absolute inability to "reflect" anything as it is "out there." It is the most creatively vital process of life at its very core.

It is not possible even for any snowflake to be identical to another, as in the world of minuscule ever-new instants our entire existence is never identically and perfectly the same.

How can the Self be able to recognize itself in this Flux? Attempts to answer this question have been made solely through convenient references to the mighty Creator's own power and will. Although it is rather absurd to think that the Creator would channel his infinite inspiration to create the ultimately silly mess we make of our lives, we choose to excuse ourselves for our self-inflicted troubles and avoid learning, wondering, and thinking any further on our own. However, our weaknesses teach us something grand about our existence as human beings.

Since prehistoric times, we have attempted to "reproduce" the design of nature as a model at the level of human interpretation. Specifically, based on our highly limited perception of physical sight, we continue to serve our observations of what we call "the world" and even construct the "perfect" order of "things" around us to explain for ourselves our constantly challenging experiences of all kinds.

As we begin and continue recognizing our abilities through our vision, based on what we see through physical sensory organs, we discover how limited, illusive, and deceiving our impressions of human reality are. We realize that by fashioning our models based on what mother nature creates, we simply produce caricatured man-made machines, only mimicking mighty nature while missing out on its creative abilities within timelessly unstoppable and unpredictable Flux. We express what we feel and see in our specific ways as human beings through the sciences, poetry, arts, music, and philosophy. However, we curiously ignore something in our picturesque and playful mental theater of consciousness: the powers that are igniting, animating, and turning absolutely invisible in their natural instances of change into spectacles that we may eventually observe. There is no way to stop the worlds of Flux, especially in our observations. We cannot ever sense or know beyond what we are.

The ancient Greek sage Heraclitus described this fundamental condition of universal existence as Flux. Observations, knowledge, or any impressions of our human experience do not exist on their own "out there," and nothing can be "reflected from out there" as it is. What we call "perceiving" is the only possible way to interact with and sense the world around us and thus digest information, revealing for us a vital process of life under the powers of the fundamental laws of irreversible instant change. Flux transformations allow our unique living beings not only to somehow interact within "outer" existences of myriad worlds and eventually randomly feel our primary interactions within and without, but moreover, to be able to instinctively transform ourselves along with our primary and invisible sensations into visions, observations, knowledge, and beliefs.

Every living mind has its own creative abilities for the sake of its very existence. My humble message for a believer is that God grants you your blessed freedom to choose to create your own realities within all the abundance and challenges of the worlds while learning from your spiritual parent to create, thus discovering the wisdom of endless vitality.

Since early childhood, we all intuitively sense metamorphic instances of what we instinctively feel as vibrations or transformations within ourselves; however, we begin to ignore this deeply intuitive sensation of unavoidable instability as we grow up. In human society, we choose not to notice the greatest power of Flux, which the sage of antiquity, Heraclitus, described as the most colossal and unavoidable condition of the world. This fundamental condition is the source of all conditions in the entirety of our everyday experiences, calculations, and experiments, and, moreover, in our modeling of all types of man-made structures that we presumably imagine to represent reality, may or shall be crudely simplified to satisfy our deduced understanding and judgment.

I invite my curious reader—and I hope to find one or two—to discover *how* the very creation of what we see as the Earth reality embraced by the universe occurs within each unique mind.

The mind's production can be expressed in myriad ways based on our observations as human beings, but our expressions cannot reflect even the tiniest fragment of the mighty world as it is. How can we ever manage to do that if the magnificent world of Flux cannot repeat any of its unique instants? The instants of the endless metamorphoses of the world have no time or space to keep handy for us to measure our ideas of time and space.

The question of why the entire existence of the instantly new myriad worlds of which we are unaware has such an ephemeral nature remains unanswered in our existing collective knowledge.

In the following chapters, the first step toward an independent search as to *how* in the first place we *are able* to exist as sovereign selves and sense, observe, memorize, and think in this world of endless, instantly appearing, and disappearing metamorphic existences.

What kinds of abilities are we granted by the nature of the magnificent Flux to be able to live as individual beings without completely melting down into forever new and unique moments within the endlessly ephemeral worlds of unstoppable change?

I believe that our primary abilities in life are unavoidably and naturally authentically creative or artistic and serve a much greater purpose than what is usually understood as creativity in the arts. These internal primary abilities allow every living being to *be*, while surviving and evolving as a more or less unique individual, along with the unique circumstances of endless change. Having these inborn abilities makes it easy for us to discover and begin to comprehend by watching the process of how we perceive what we believe reality is.

We are unable even to sense anything unless the inborn living **mechanism of perception** in our minds is "at work," transforming our primary and yet invisible instances of interactions into our unique internal compositions of realities that we observe as playhouses within our minds. How does this creative mechanism function and reveal itself?

Any living mind is a little creator of a unique self, as it can intuitively reproduce itself within entirely changing and ceaselessly transforming environments.

Whether gifted or not, we never exist as exactly the same identical units, as it would be impossible for us— unique beings—to face and sense exactly repetitive conditions and challenges. Therefore, we cannot have exactly the same experiences, knowledge, or ideas. We are amazingly free to learn and live through intimate, unique, and ever-changing experiences, whether all that may seem to us is more or less "the same."

The most fundamental reasons for our existence are within ourselves, but we often fail to recognize them. Anyone can discover the essence of oneself, and this adventure is what we here embark on, forming the basis of this study and described in the following notes.

Why is it that nothing and no one can be treated in the exact same way as our societies, politicians, industrialists, and medical professionals often insist on, for the sake of serving the same rigid manmade rules and laws by crudely adjusting living beings to non-existing dull collective prototypes impossible in the living world?

Every single life is blessed from its birth with the primordial freedom to be its unique Self, created within its internal and sovereign mind's residence.

No real balance, exact equality, equity, identical copies of anything, repetitions, symmetry, perfect reversal, conservation of mass or anything else, or absolute isolation is ever possible under the colossal powers of Flux. Every life entity is unique within itself, as this is the only way to exist as a single self, as well as facilitate the existence of many selves. Absolute copies would absorb one another and cease to exist under the mighty powers of Flux. In our worlds of instant metamorphosis, we are always dealing with—in ways more or less practical for us—*approximations of our experiences*, never with any sort of exactness other than in our imagination. Why is it that our perceptions are forever crude, and therefore, we all imagine "the same thing"?

While reading the first chapter of this work, one can easily discover the crucially vital nature of **the very process of perceiving conditions ignited by Flux within oneself**—and how under these conditions we build our experiences and knowledge, but only from what we are able to perceive and compose.

To absolutely know *something*, we must entirely become this very *something*, losing the uniqueness of our original selves.

We have a wonderful ability to *Compare* our perceptions with our previous experiences. No life is possible without the ability to *Compare* sensations. The primitive visions that we depict, observe, analyze, calculate, and prove or disprove are based on strictly limited human corporeal perceptions, which we somehow may record and collect as impressions. Even our impressions cannot be frozen and stay perfectly unchanged even for a moment, though we may not notice any changes for a while. The training in our education systems and established systematic methods of obtaining knowledge curiously demonstrate and characterize rather rigid habits to be followed in patterns of thinking, rather than a true vital assimilation of experiences. The habit of following patterns is often called professionalism. This can work and even be helpful in some cases unless our ever-changing environments surprise us with the unexpected tasks.

We cannot avoid our very process of perceiving as a continuous, exclusively internal mental process. The "things" or events are invisible to us until they are uniquely turned in each of our minds into more or less unique mental productions. However, nothing produced in our minds can be visible or sensed outside our minds as these visions have been originally and internally produced.

We communicate by expressing our experiences by symbolically assembling our collectively rendered images, sounds, language, opinions, and prototypes based on our presumably similar experiences. This is how we mistake our collective opinions and symbolic images for "objective" reality, and commonly use these to prove an "objective" truth and even knowledge.

Can objective reality that is "out there" fit in our minds as it is?

The "tangible" or physical realities we may sense are not "objective," not "out there," as they are impossible on their own unless we process our own primary non-physical sensations into uniquely tangible and even visible subjects in each of our minds. The playful appearances of impressions we perceive through the unique bodily organs called eyes, or what we term sight, have been extensively researched and described as shallow and deceiving. Sifted through the bodily organs these appearances are made possible, but they are not inside the physical bodily organs. The perceiver and producer of visions are our ephemeral minds, responsible for processing our unique momentary sensations into thoughts, feelings, and appearances. Sadly, the possible explanations for these illusive visions formed in our minds we commonly mistake for objective reality. Truly convincing explanations of this phenomenon have been missing in our history of research and, to this day, in the entirety of the contemporary sciences. How does this occur?

To explain the illusiveness of our sight, on which we rely our knowledge, one must finally dare to ask, *How* in the first place does all of what we see and analyze get into our own minds? Why is it that no images or thoughts can be found in any of the physical organs especially the brain? The bodily organs cannot observe or think on their own.

Where is the mind "located," the thinking, memorizing, dreaming, fantasizing, sensing, and feeling mind, which moreover *observes* objects and events, brains and bodies, other living beings, or universal landscapes?

We now begin to enter the unknown field of our mind to discover ourselves in it while bringing our learning further along from where the great sages and philosophers of ancient Greece left off.

Although deeply intuitive philosophers in our history have contemplated and articulated the impossibility of us reflecting anything as it is "out there," such notions have not been explained and are highly inconvenient for us to even admit and to accept in our contemporary schools of learning.

Despite observing and experiencing our manmade staged theater of societies, constituting habits, rules, and orders that we try to follow with great difficulty, we naively believe that we live in an open world.

As we begin to discover for ourselves, and within ourselves, the most magnificent fundamental natural law of *Flux*, and our inborn abilities to perceive our unique realities, the confounding human notion of "reflecting" reality "out there," especially within our brains, would prove absolutely futile.

Can we furnish a physical organ, called the brain, with objects as they are out there?

Again, *how* is it possible for us to perceive and observe memories and think, imagine, and feel some *differences* in what we observe? We are about to discover our *perceptions,* not as mirror-like flattish reflections imprinted on our brains, but as the most vivid of nature's tools for sensing and *processing* our lives within ourselves.

We may see similarities in thinking between the contemporary sciences and the lovely and well-known expressions in the arts and poetry, such as William Blake's poetry, where he describes our eyes as "open windows" to the world. Another poetical quote by Blake sounds as contemporary as scientific beliefs regarding future technologies: "If the doors of perception were cleansed, everything would appear to man as it is infinite" (featured in the work *The Marriage of Heaven and Hell* by the English poet and printmaker William Blake).

However, Marcel Proust suggested, somewhat more daringly, *"The real voyage of discovery consists, not in seeking new landscapes, but in having new eyes."* "La Prisonnière," the fifth volume of "Remembrance of Things Past" (also known as) "In Search of Lost Time."

Nonetheless, how can a mind sense and perceive visions on its own when using no physical eyes, ears, brain, or any other corporeal sensory organs of a body in dreams, thinking, or imagining?

I would further encourage you to understand Proust's "new eyes" metaphorically, as a suggestion to find a new, even drastically different perception of not physical eyes but the mind's eye contemplating its internal mental existence.

Therefore, we seek a new field of experience. We have more precious undiscovered findings ahead—our as-yet unappreciated gifts of nature for life. I suggest the pursuit of unconventional research beginning from the most vital functions of our mind driven by nature's vital ***mechanism of perceptions***.

I would not be surprised to face conventional criticism resting on the same old-fashioned and stubbornly rigid patterns of thinking, habits, and behavior that are misleading our society to remain unaware of the mighty laws of nature that seemingly no one is able to circumvent. The permanently immeasurable and absolutely untouchable powers of *Flux* crush this human ignorance. Restrictiveness in the sciences that we are taught leaves new findings of all types that are poorly explained and are only sorted out by labeled categories. Within established patterns of thinking, the possibility of fundamental discoveries to find new solutions to solve our problems would never be possible.

Can we ever hope to evolve as authentically creative species in the amazing conditions of ephemeral Flux? Pursuing our still-primitive human desires to capture, use, and abuse everything we think is possible to reach, to "know" by mindlessly manipulating, fixing, or destroying the unknown life for the sake of artificial temporary conveniences, comforts, and fashions, we have built thick walls of "progress" blocking us from wisely learning about coexistence within natural environments that are ever new to us, the only conditions where we may coherently evolve ourselves.

However, we are just a step or two away from discovering *how* to at least begin to creatively evolve.

Our unique human minds interact with the ever-changing temporary vessels of our physical bodies, which are taking us on a journey that we call physical experience. By sensing these unique interactions, we can learn that the formations of living organisms are not truly "solid" entities, and we can see through the modest achievements in the sciences that bodies are combinations of living cells, atoms, viruses, bacteria, tissues, and other microscopic organisms that form bodily parts and sensory organs. We can also see that everything within the vessel of a body has its internal environment, and, as contemporary scientific knowledge states, ninety-nine percent of the human body is made up of carbon, hydrogen, nitrogen, and oxygen atoms, along with those of other chemical elements.

One might wonder, "Is this me? Who am I—cells, atoms, viruses in water? How can I be my Self surviving among so many different organisms composing a body that I strangely interact with and feel, but which I do not truthfully know at all?" Are these bodies things-in-themselves? How do we sense them?

Through such contemplations, one's deep intuition reveals that one possesses a Self, a living mind, a spirit, a soul, allowing one to be an entity and be able to willingly observe, think, memorize, and even more or less comprehend one's own existence. However, is it possible to explain *how* a bodyless *mind manages to sense on its own*, whether using a corporeal body or not, and above all, to exist creatively and sense itself without the eyes, ears, brain, or any other bodily sensory organs?

However, when temporary bodies are disconnected from sensations in the mind, they become paralyzed, fall apart, and die.

The new field of discovery is beyond the deceiving landscapes that we are observing at the stage of the mind's playful and constantly fluctuating theatrical spectacles. What we call consciousness is awaiting for our step, beyond its curtains. We observe our shallow spectacles of consciousness only as long as our minds intuitively sift our mental sensations while interacting through our bodily organs, especially in relation to sight.

Taking a step beyond the thick curtains of the flattish consciousness of our mind might be quite a challenging adventure for us with our conventional thinking patterns.

In contemporary schools, before undergoing training in grammar and math, no student has the opportunity to acquire basic knowledge about *how we manage to see what we see*. *Why* is it that the physical organs called the eyes cannot actually see on their own?

The first explanation is that we observe some appearances, but only internally, after perceiving and processing invisible momentary sensations. We must perceive/process our sensations because we may never sense anything directly as it is "out there." We are limited. Our observing abilities rely on an internal mental process, which we are about to discover. Why these limitations though? Is this a curse or a protective gift from mother nature showing the reason for why we are unable to reflect our environments as we so wish, directly?

If one could miraculously fly outside of oneself just to see realities outside of oneself objectively, the colossal powers of Flux creating endlessly new transformations would melt one down, in no time, as a tiny lump of sugar in a hot cup of tea. Every living mind has its unique *limitations*, not just for challenging obstacles, but initially to serve every single life as great **protective boundaries**.

First, Newtonian or Einsteinian laws and conditions, or any other classical theories described in physics, chemistry, biology, or mathematics, are not universal natural laws. These conditions and our explanations following our physical laws only indicate our specific and limited human experience, which is mainly affected by our unique bodily sensations and our specific mental perceptions of these corporeal temporary sensations. These sensations of what we recognize as physical have been processed in our minds, but mainly come from our bodily sensory organs and their interactions in the limited, not objective, surrounding environments.

In other words, these physical impressions are based on conditions of our bodies, which we mistakenly imagine are providing reflections of "objective" reality through sensory abilities such as corporeal sight.

Ironically, the proof of these "realities" found through the sciences is mainly based upon recorded appearances perceived through this very corporeal sight, which is known in the field of psychology of human perception to be the most deceptive, illusive, tricky, and superficial sensory perception of all those we may possess. The sciences must thoroughly revise their outdated methods of observing and understanding natural design, which are limited by learning from only superficial appearances in our theatrical consciousness. While mainly depending on the appearances augmented through super microscopes or super telescopes, built after our physical eyes, our visions are unavoidably "lending" on stages of our superficial consciousness.

Why is it that our technology does not manifest the true presence of human intelligence but, on the contrary, reveals how poor human abilities are constantly challenged within fluctuating environmental conditions? Technologies today serve more or less as crutches for human beings who cannot fly, run, or swim fast enough, and who cannot develop protective fur, shells, or feathers. Humans poorly see, hear or smell when compared to the majority of animals. Our use of our technologies shows how extremely needy and eventually helpless we become as human beings, both physically and mentally.

What critical understanding is still missing from our knowledge of our existence? To recognize the most powerful and absolutely unavoidable conditions of the world, which are present in our mundane life—in our visions or dreams, memories, and thinking—whether we categorize our experience as common, artistic, scientific, philosophical, physical, or mental—we do not need any technology.

It is very important to admit that everything we may observe in the superficial stages of what we recognize as human "consciousness" is already instinctively *processed through our very limited sensory perceptions.*

Imagine that our consciousness is actually highly superficial, similar to the flat screens of computers and TVs, such that our perceptions catch our primary "sparks" of sensations as signals on the surface of a somewhat flattish consciousness. The sensations in our mind consciousness work like the signals or "pixels" that are composed on a computer screen. The mind processes instances of sensations into compositions of appearances that are observable to us within.

As we focus on human physical or bodily organs they are resembling us some organic "devices." These remain greatly under-developed, and unlike animals and other living beings in the wild, when we greatly depend on these organs, we are very poorly coordinated in life, in the wilderness, and even in our artificial "isolation" from numerous natural conditions that we build within our communities, villages, towns, and cities as long as for millennia, and commuting via artificial road systems with road signs for easy communication suitable for human needs. Except for human beings, no form of life needs maps, compasses, clocks, clothing, manufactured food, Wi-Fi, automobiles, jets, rockets, or any other technology for communication, nor do they need artificially produced energy, artificial entertainment, "weather reports," or the "news." Even when we try very hard to compensate for our great human limitations and obstacles in life by building artificial devices augmenting our corporeal sight or hearing, as well as building complicated but rather clumsy vessels for sea, air, and space travel, when compared to nature's original living design, these super-gadgets remain primitive and unsafe, and the same problems remain as our bodies are not naturally equipped with faculties for flying or swimming etc., on their own. Manipulating our bodies to the extreme as we do is abysmally unwise when we compare this with an appreciation for the innate skill and aptitude of nature's creations.

With our great pride in all our technological achievements, we only become more opinionated rather than truly knowledgeable—and in many cases, while depending on tech gadgets, our minds become lazier; we are subject to nature's ever-changing conditions and challenges, but we hardly notice them until disasters "suddenly" Strike. For instance, while using wireless gadgets, we can now reach each other across great distances but still cannot understand each other any better than we could millennia ago. We continue to argue, fight, and mindlessly destroy things as living beings trying to manipulate nature's design and struggle to replace it lacking a true understanding of what we are dealing with.

Our artificial human language, based on conventionally assembled systems of symbols, images, and sounds that form words and images of words, requires training to be perceived, understood, and used as a supposedly meaningful form of communication. This remains the prevailing method of sharing our seemingly collective ideas. However, nothing can be perceived or understood directly and perfectly in the same way that others perceive and understand it; our perceptions are unique. Do we need to relearn to communicate among ourselves? When we exchange our experiences through artificially invented and established languages consisting of uniform groups of signs, symbols, sounds, and images, our personal living experiences are easily misunderstood, and the original meaning is twisted in different ways within different minds. We are not born speaking our man-made languages but have to learn them by mimicking adults. Perhaps mimicking abilities prevail over all the other abilities that many of us may possess.

Before expressing ourselves in human language, we must hear, see, and process symbolic words in our personal imagination while preliminarily reviewing the meanings of these language symbols in our minds. We also try to predict some actions, our own and those of others, by playing scenarios in our imagination before we speak and act. Thus, it takes seconds, or much longer, to articulate our thoughts or feelings, especially when we compare our own language-based communications to immediate instinctive communications among other forms of life, spontaneously exchanging intuitive sensations they are personally experiencing within natural environments and commonly in any distances.

Under the most powerful law of *Flux*, nothing can be truly and absolutely left unchanged, reflected, copied, repeated, or duplicated. We change entirely while we interact and communicate.

There is no equality or equity for all, but endless possibilities of creative harmonious coexistence for the sake of vitality. This is the fundamental condition of God's creative nature.

No man-made law is truly powerful enough to withstand nature's power.

The world of *Flux* is an endlessly harmonious orchestra against cacophonies, where we learn to sense and recognize it, listen to it, and make our choices. Whether we are gifted with good ears and sing along as wondrous single instruments or carelessly produce loud cacophonies destroying ourselves and screaming in desperation until we lose our own singing voices, we are all granted some blessed creative abilities that are hidden deeply inside us. These blessed abilities are tuned to the vitality of nature, leading us to safety and meaningful survival.

We are naturally born with deep primary intuition, similar to all other living beings. Intuition, like an internal compass in our intimately ever-new and ever-changing environment, leads us to act in accordance with change.

As we grow up, we begin to suppress this inborn intuition. Starting from our early childhood training, education, and practice in mimicking adults, we become little players in the societal playhouse, struggling to fit and serve stiff man-made structures and systems. It is debatable whether our human society is still tribal or more complex, or whether we have developed our wisdom based on our beliefs or have borrowed knowledge from other older cultures and only manipulated it, mindlessly abusing the original meaning, into instructions that are sometimes extreme and cultish; nonetheless, as soon as we are trained enough to adapt to these artificial constructs that unify and control our beliefs, minds, bodies, and lifestyles, we find ourselves locked up inside confusing and even destructive human activities. We commonly mistake what we observe and see for the objective world, and then our world becomes too small as we are struggling to fit man-made culture, systems, models, and judgments.

In the first place, however, our sensory perceptions are not designed to directly see, touch, or hear anything as it is. If we were directly exposed to everything, as mentioned above, we would melt away in no time in a world of ever-changing instants. We need our specific limitations, which are conditions that I suggest we should view not just as obstacles, but as **protective boundaries** for life.

We are here to discover comprehensive explanations for the fascinating nature of our world and keep discovering the as-yet ungrasped Flux itself, the most vital source of our existence. Even with our limited ability to perceive our realities, we can still deeply sense some new irreversible conditions within and without. However, no one can reflect on anything just as it is, as nothing remains as it was exactly an instant ago.

Yet, how do we actually recognize ourselves, "separating" ourselves from the rest of the spectacles, backgrounds, and objects that are visible to us? Why is it that we ourselves are never objective observers?

These questions can be answered in our new field of knowledge of the nature of the mind, showing its endless wonders and possibilities as we begin to comprehend and explore ourselves in unexampled or unparalleled ways.

To understand, learn about, and evolve our minds, we need to begin by carefully revising our existing basic education, which lacks the very foundation of knowledge we are yet to build. To establish new cross-sector interactive schools for sharing experiences, learning, and practicing our innovative approach toward advanced education, no capital such as accumulated wealth or money is needed. Classical gatherings for education, such as in ancient schools where teachers and students of all sorts and interests gather to exchange what they know and think together, can be organized anywhere.

"The sun is new each day," as the great sage Heraclitus asserted, explaining the concept of Flux as early as c. 535–475 BC. Heraclitus is the most profound thinker in our short history; his teachings continue to enlighten us with fundamental knowledge of the nature of the world and the most powerful laws we may experience in it. However, he has not been understood for millennia. It is very inconvenient for us, as humans, to accept the obvious fact that change is instantly "transforming" us, our minds, and bodies, into new minds and bodies before we can blink. Though Flux is an unavoidable condition everywhere, and we watch our stubborn struggle to build permanent, fixed, and balanced systems or manufacture "perfect things"—dreaming about unbreakable societies under man-made rules, all that is destined to be doomed even before we begin to build them. Small diverse systems are easy to fix and improve when they are interactive; if they collapse, we replace them locally with better varieties without causing great destruction to the earth, as colossal artificially built systems unavoidably do.

Before we can even sense something, the magnificent world of Flux entirely transforms it into an entirely new ephemeral composition. We have no time to notice the metamorphic existence of the world we inhabit.

Our uniquely limited perceptions of our realities allow us to interpret our circumstances and become responsible for our own existence. Our interacting "tools" are our *perceptions* manifesting the existence of our life—that is the most creative *process* we may ever experience and know.

The unthinkable Flux keeps affecting our minds and bodies beyond our comprehension, as the world is perpetually changing its conditions within less than an instant; it cannot "wait" and "freeze" itself to allow us to see, photograph, or record and store any segment of it in any permanent format, not even in our fantasies, which must instantly change to continue our dreams and thoughts. We observe only our own limitedly rendered impressions of realities we may experience.

I believe that our basic artistic abilities are granted to us by nature for a much greater purpose than to create art as we know it. Our sensations are living colorful paints, our feelings are brushes, and our intuition empowers the artist's creative Self. The mind is an artist, always in the process of interpreting what it senses as events, characters, landscapes, and even animated stories. No photography or video technology can replace the artistic abilities internally granted to us to create ourselves freely from the core of our characters. The intuitive and fertile creativity of a living mind is the source of life.

The mind creates from what it perceives, from hopelessly poor vision to magnificent spectacles. **Nature's living mechanism of perceptions** propels our unique realities.

This primordial mental *mechanism of perceptions* has been unnoticed for millennia, but it amusingly demonstrates its routine in the process of painting a classical work of art. While painting, a classical artist constantly **compares,** *selects, and focuses* on something that seems important, overlaying it on a vague background of the mind. The artist then *frames* his finished work, separating it from all disturbances created by the surroundings of all sorts; our minds operate similarly. This explains why we perceive our realities similarly.

Painting on flat surfaces is guided by the deep intuitive behavior of the mind. That is, the theatrical consciousness that we develop on the stages of our imagination is separated from the depths of our minds. Every mind goes through the classical artist's routine, and this instinctive mental routine is endlessly present in us, whether we are observing, thinking about, memorizing, or imagining something, or whether we are awake or asleep.

We are taking a step into the unknown field of the mind's nature, heading toward a new era of breakthrough discoveries that can neither fit inside labs nor actual brains, cannot be explained by fixed equations, and cannot be detected through any man-made device.

We are about to discover our mind's natural abilities responsible for creating its visualization in "consciousness," where our pictorial imagination thrives, while building its fantastic scenarios of what we sense and understand as our realities. While we are watching our primary sensations, *nature's mechanism of perceptions allows us to Compare, Select, Compose, Focus, and even "frame" our mental productions.* Perception is a principal drive creating all our visions. The very process of perception eventually empowers all our feelings and sensations of life.

Nature's mechanism of perceptions is what all forms of life have in common, that is, in our mutual instinctive effort to thrive and survive within the conditions of the unstoppable Flux.

Every life change is limited in many ways, and our limitations play a crucial role in revealing nature's wonders of **protective boundaries** saving our existence from complete dissolution into the overwhelming powers of Flux, whether we are aware of these **protective boundaries**, or take these as obstacles or even a curse. Only a few notes remain from the great philosopher of antiquity, Protagoras, on his contemplations of *limitations* as an inseparable crucial function of the entire condition of Flux. His writings were banned and eventually destroyed by the authorities of his time.

To further develop the fundamental and immortal thoughts of thinkers such as Heraclitus and Protagoras on the unavoidable laws of universal nature, I suggest beginning with contemplation of *nature's living mechanism of perceptions, within our own mind,* which reveals to us why our entire existence is inseparable from and depends entirely on the instant and irreversible worlds of playhouses of creative nature.

Our human history is still at the dawn of its evolution.

I invite every curious reader—and I still hope to find one or two—to join this pioneering study beyond the closed "spaces" of existing institutions, laboratories, and technologies, beyond exciting appearances through super microscopes or telescopes where the long-outdated, entangled, and confused human knowledge has been recycling while misleading our psyche, mentalities, ideas, and deeds for millennia.

V. NOVA

CHAPTER ONE

The Natural Mechanism of Perceptions within the Unavoidable Laws of *Flux*

In this chapter, I would like to share a discovery that struck me in a most unprecedented way. At that time, I was still a teen artist and not able to find any knowledge of this "artistic" behavior of my mind anywhere. It took me some time to find out that this kind of knowledge did not exist.

While painting a still life in my art class in an old academic art school, I noticed that while depicting my work on canvas, I kept comparing, selecting, focusing, and composing images in my mind repeatedly while painting them on my canvas.

I noticed that I kept following this as a sort of routine, first in my mind, instinctively, as all artists do; however, I received no school instruction of this kind.

I then had to admit that my mind unstoppably explored this artist's routine beyond my comprehension, while *observing, memorizing, learning, thinking, calculating,* and *dreaming,* whether I was awake or asleep.

I first wondered whether I was subnormal, but after thinking about this idea day and night and watching other people, I had to conclude that none of us could stop comparing, selecting, focusing, and composing our impressions of our environments into ever-changing visions, just like a painter. All that we do begins with mental activities of various sorts. Even when suffering a sudden bodily injury, the mind cannot immediately sense pain. Rather, the mind takes time to instinctively process the initial sensations of its interaction with the body affected by the pain. Pain, joy, and all the other primary sensations related to bodies must first be perceived in the mind.

Something then grabbed my attention in that art class. Why is this very easily noticeable artist's routine, which has been used instinctively or intuitively for millennia in prehistoric and traditional art, never been recognized as a major function of the mind? This unstoppable mental artist's routine activates our senses. Without it, we cannot perceive, communicate, memorize, think, or dream. Each living mind behaves as a subconscious or primordial artist in every one of us, activating the very process of its existence and making it intimately and uniquely personal within oneself.

I decided to share my overwhelmed thoughts with my art teacher. I was painfully shy when tried to clumsily explain that art is not a human invention. Our minds must possess inborn, instinctive abilities to observe reality in a manner similar to the routines that all artists follow while painting. Our minds clearly demonstrate what kind of mental processes literally _makes_ us see, think, memorize, imagine, and dream. Just like any classically trained painter, our deeply instinctive minds keep **comparing, selecting, focusing,** and _composing_ randomly selected subjects and images of what we believe we look at "out there." In our minds, we "frame" subjects of our observation in groups, just as we frame thoughts by isolating them from the rest of what we keep in our minds. In this way, we strive to create some sort of order in our minds to make things observable in a coherent composition. As we need to compare what we sense, we easily discover that we cannot see just one thing separately on its own, unrelated to anything else. This is how our minds unstoppably create their internal environment by connecting not only sensations but also visions as groups of multiple images, as well as combinations of thoughts and ideas, including seemly restrictive mathematics and the sciences, philosophy, and literature. The artist's routine is unavoidable. As it is impossible for us to truly see anything separately on its own, we must instinctively "shoot" and continuously change our focus on what attracts or disturbs us, putting the rest to linger in a deep vague background. One can recognize how memories emerge from these lingering backgrounds of our living thoughts.

Why do we perceive in spite of we still never see anything as it is "out there?" The clearest thoughts in philosophy over the past several hundred years have been led by the intuitively brilliant logic of George Berkeley on the idea of a "thing in itself," discussed in his 1713 work _Three Dialogues Between Hylas and Philonous._ (Immanuel Kant only borrowed Berkeley's original idea of a "thing in itself").

After his pioneering philosophical writing, _Three Dialogues Between Hylas and Philonous,_ Berkeley simply stopped thinking about any further explanation. He only refers everything to the Creator's _will._ I think, however, despite Berkeley's idea that the Creator puts everything in our minds, exploring all the grand creative powers _He_ possesses, it is impossible that the Creator would bother to put countless mundane, silly, pretty, ugly, bloody, confusing, or simply stupid visions and ideas in our minds. Therefore, I posit that it is easier to understand why we are so generously granted the wondrous tools of perception, that allow us to be free to learn to create on our own as little creators. We can discover and learn from our natural basic abilities to create our visions looking for our ways in our ever-changing existence. The mind is a little creator for the sake of its vitality.

We cannot observe anything directly and instantly, and we cannot set things or living beings in our minds just as they are out there. "Things in themselves" neither fit our minds, nor brains. Even the physical sensations that we think we effortlessly feel must somehow be assimilated. We are able to observe only what we are able to mentally process or digest through perception. Our visions are unique impressions composed of our experiences, together with ever-changing sensations emerging like the instant sparks of living energies. What we feel as "material" or "physical" is the result of our mental work, affected by temporary crude and random interactions with what we observe as a "physical" body, which is an organic composition of myriads of different life forms. These forms of life contain living minds on their own.

Whether rich or poor, our minds are "cooking" not only what we perceive and sense as our reality but also producing the impressions we express in symbolic forms, similar to expressions of the primordial artist who at first has processed his creative imagination in his mind before depicting it on the flattish surfaces of his cave walls. Symbolic or simplified images form shows the first stage of human language development.

When affected by the conditions of the body, the mind creates its internal, temporary, theatrical, and superficial "consciousness" of spectacles, where the body is acting as a visible entity to the mind, as long as it can sense a body.

This means that only the mind is the creator of visions of its "reality universes," and no brain or any other bodily organ is able to compose and observe any of our visions. Our minds are responsible for processing all our ever-fluctuating sensations. Whether while receiving bodily signals or on their own, our minds follow their subconscious routine behavior of *comparing, selecting, focusing, composing, and framing* initial abstract impressions and sensations, and as an artist turning them into visions. Just like any art pieces these can be poor, silly, funny, horrific, or harmoniously beautiful. No surgeon, researcher, or butcher has ever seen any image, thought, word, or number in a brain. The brain is only a bodily sensory organ and cannot perceive on its own. You can enjoy, or be healed, or destroyed by what your mind can stage for you.

Unlike an artist, the mind cannot stop *comparing, selecting, focusing, and composing*, whether we are awake, asleep, dreaming, thinking, or memorizing. This process is inseparable from the existence of ourselves as selves. *It reveals that the blessed act of perceiving is the most basic process of life.* By willingly changing our mind's perceptions based on our experiences, we may be able to greatly enrich, revive, and reinvent our very existence.

A few days after thinking over this young artist's unprecedented observation, I told my art teacher: "I think that the mind is a primordial artist living within ourselves."

As we fail to recognize our internal abilities of perception, we fail to grasp the very process of observing and thinking.

We try to express ourselves through human language, behavior, and what we call ideas, rendered in the arts, sciences, or philosophy, with no clue about what makes our realities possible for us. The ***living mechanism of perceptions*** remains hidden behind the curtains of our temporary mental theater of superficial human consciousness, where we prefer to observe and judge the appearances of what we believe reality is.

These realities are unique products of our minds' perceptions and interpretations of our life experiences of ourselves. One mind is one interpreter of life for each person.

Whether we believe that we may see the actual world with gods and aliens, monsters and angels, or robotic systems independently floating in the universe, our sensations are strictly personal, unique instances of our primary and abstract interactions, without and within our minds. We cannot ever repeat instances of our lives, but in different ways, we do create our expressions of what we uniquely feel and experience. Judging the world based on our impressions processed in our temporary theatrical consciousness would keep us in the dark ages of recurring human history.

The world is difficult to understand in terms of *Flux* for adults; however, this great ancient philosophical notion is still inborn and roving in each of our minds since infancy, when we still were newcomers from another "dimension" and did not have to become great philosophers to sense the majestic transformations of everything inside and around us.

Heraclitus's timeless discovery, which he articulates in his poetic depictions of the colossal *Flux*, is an unavoidable condition of all conditions.

For the first time, I suggest trying to comprehend the deeply intuitive *mechanism of perception of our minds interacting* with the metamorphosis of *Flux*.

We commonly recognize our mind as the soul or spirit, whose natural functions now explain, based on a process of perception, how endlessly creative our possibilities may become.

The mechanism of perceptions is not mechanical, but its functions can nonetheless be explained clearly, as we may feel them instinctively in every moment. Based on this most essential mental process of assimilating our primary, immediate, and instantly immerging sensations, from which every mind builds its wonders of existence, each living entity recognizes its reality after some experience has already been uniquely staged within its mind. Every form of life that we commonly observe, even just as the appearance of some physical body, possesses a unique mind, which creates its intimate personal and unique reality.

What can be a more precious gift from God for a believer than the blessed freedom to exist and evolve as your Self while learning to create and exploring your inborn abilities of a little creator? Granted the freedom to create and recreate oneself one is learning about the world after the wisdom of one's spiritual parent. If you fail, try again under any condition. Each life is originally thriving in a living process of self-development or evolution, and these possibilities are open not only to every one of us human beings but also to all life forms.

As living beings, we can build unique sovereign realities and characters that no one but ourselves can truly destroy.

Back in my art class, I remember how, after I spoke with my kind art teacher trying to think over my new clumsy but striking teenage observations. I was unable to accurately articulate my overwhelming experience. My art teacher knew that I had been studying classical philosophy since I was 11 years old and he loved discussing classical and contemporary ideas in art and life with me. However, that new conversation about the nature of our perceptions working together as an ephemeral mechanism within our minds felt very special for both of us. A few days later, my art teacher told me that he believed I was not only a promising art student but also a little philosopher and that I should write down my ideas, at least as notes, no matter how clumsy these notes might be. I followed his thoughtful advice and have never regretted it. From that very day, I started writing down on random pieces of paper and even napkins—my abbreviated thoughts, which I later developed in the work *An Artist's Notes*.

Something that is new and unknown is extremely difficult to formulate in common language or a traditional professional format. It is much easier to criticize new thoughts by gluing them to categories of already known topics discovered by previously established authors. I presume that my work will never be accepted as is. However, I have noticed that the truly pioneering works in history were never beautifully or perfectly expressed and performed. In the fields of mathematics, physics, research, literature, and philosophy, as well as in classical art, innovative works did not look as greatly polished, organized, and refined as the works of their followers, who did not need to discover or invent anything new again but could instead work on polishing new skills in their presentation of others' remarkable ideas, as revealed by the original pioneers.

How do we learn while exploring our perception of *comparison*, and why is it critical? While our young, still very clumsy, bodies are developing, and before we take our first steps on the ground and pronounce our first words, we intuitively begin to explore our inborn talents of a primordial creative artist. This artist is already residing within our ephemeral young minds.

A very young child swims in an endless ocean of instant-by-instant sensations. Not just Heraclitus but every living being has this primordial experience from birth. As one's mind feels its first impressions through new interactions with a tiny newly developing body, one keeps comparing one's first vague abstract sensations while still becoming familiar with one's somewhat alien, young, and undeveloped body.

The instinct of *comparison* is a primary function of every living being, and that is why a human *mind* slowly learns to feel its child's body that needs years to grow up "physically," still learning how to explore bodily functional sensory organs to see, hear, and collate one's first corporeal impressions, through this yet "unexperienced" young body with one head, one mouth, one nose, two ears, two eyes, two legs, and two arms, etc. Nature has granted us these living tools for exploring our existence in manifold ways.

It takes time for the mind of an infant to be able to sense the world through its physical organs, such as the eyes, while differentiating its still-blurry impressions of the mother's hand, comparing it with her lips and her voice pronouncing unfamiliar words filled with love. The first non-physical mentally perceived sensations that penetrate the young body are striking.

Mental *comparison* is our most vital, basic ability in life; while perceiving a very young body, it animates our so-called entirely new (to the young individual) physical movements based on our sensations and feelings. This physical experience may be shocking at first, occurring at a stage when we cannot yet talk. Thus, babies cry.

Why is it that the mental process of comparing our forever variable impressions is *unstoppable,* whether we are awake or asleep, memorizing, or thinking? If we cannot compare our mental sensations, we will feel no differences in our experiences and in our bodies, as they then become senseless and fail to exist—the death of the brain and the rest of the body follows when a mind stops *comparing bodily sensations.*

Our bodily functions become paralyzed when they are disconnected from the mind. Interactions between the mind and body mutually ignite their energies so that they act as living magnets, attracting one another. In rare cases, the deep physical stress created by our overwhelming, physical sensations storming through the body can eventually paralyze all our corporeal sensory organs and, similar to an electric shock, cause complete bodily dysfunction and physical death. While alive, our bodies are interconnected throughout affected by our mental functions, keeping our temporary bodies alive as one organism.

Constantly energized and affected by sensations, our memories are like Heraclitus' River, always running as they are transforming. However, we cannot experience the same sensations, feelings, or memories twice. Memories seemingly flow in their ephemeral moment-by-moment transformations. Memories are never fixed but are ever-changing in their flow, thus constantly transforming the rest of our Selves, just like Heraclitus' River.

Our mentally produced sensations create powerful fields that keep our realities together.

As these internal fields of primary sensations affect what we may observe and feel, they are similar to what we describe as magnetic fields in physics. No physical reality can exist on its own. Specific sensations that we experience while interacting with the world around us using our body, which we feel and call physical conditions, are not "objective conditions."

We must possess living minds to experience sensations in ever-changing formations, including the visions of magnetic fields within our minds—the perceivers. We cannot discover magnetic fields or their nature if we have no sensations. Under the power of Flux, there is no time to keep anything together in any instant composition. Flux is instantaneous metamorphosis. Our minds have the gift of composing themselves from the powers of constant change, producing unique fields of internal wonder realities.

When we begin searching for the basic functions of the mind (not the brain), we can be astonished at how the possibilities and abilities of the mind, naturally granted to every living being from birth, enable us to survive by transforming and recreating ourselves. Unlike humans, many living beings (e.g., jellyfish, corals, trees, plants, or mushrooms) do not require a brain to sense their ever-transforming environment. These transformations are deeply metamorphic as all expediencies of physical reality, its physical laws, and the "material" feelings of them, all that begins from our ephemeral fluctuating instances of mental sensations.

The greatest confusion we human beings face in dealing with life is not outside ourselves, but within.

No mind can leave itself to observe anything in the mighty world beyond itself. If one were to escape from one's self into an outer existence of the colossal powers of Flux, one would melt away like a tiny lump of sugar in a cup of very hot tea. No spaceship can ever take us outside ourselves to see the universe objectively, because a spaceship only carries bodies, moreover, we sense bodies traveling into the cosmic landscapes perceived and therefore, become visible only inside minds.

Findings in physics, chemistry, and even psychology tell us that scholars and theorists in these fields are missing the presence of themselves in all they have been observing, analyzing, and describing, commonly imagining possible objectivity in their contemplations and modeling.

First, each of our minds is a unique perceiver and *observer*. *Nature's mechanism of perceptions* of the mind eventually shows that it is not the brain that produces thoughts as a physical liver produces bile, as a popular materialistic idea proposes.

Every mind naturally possesses its primordial art, sound recording, and animation studios, all in its creative "chamber," and none of our so-called inventions, such as the visual arts, theatrical performances, movies, recordings, and technologies of any kind, are truly our human invention.

No technology or science can answer where our minds are and how our minds observe and think, creating visions of what we sense and feel as reality. As a mere bodily transmitter, the brain cannot produce an actual image or thought. Minds are not observable by other spectators.t They are observers within themselves as unique sovereign entities.

Although based on using similar physical sensory or bodily perceptions that we might sense in our *collectively described* experiences, we never truly sense anything in exactly the same way, as our minds are entirely unique to live as individual selves, not just one mind. Each of our realities has its own internal universe composed of our productions of it. Human experience cannot be objective; when combined, our information remains only approximately *collective* and *not objective*.

In protecting our own existence, as well as everything else that may exist, we experience great *limitations*. A contemporary of Heraclitus, the philosopher Protagoras, revealed and contemplated the endless limitations of everything that might exist. Limitations are just as changeable, as they are always attuned to the powers of *Flux*. Despite the world conditions of opposites (which have been described by Heraclitus), opposites are never equal, possessing a tendency toward *unbalancing* conditions of all sorts. Flux never allows any perfect balance that we dream about in our unreal models of structured systems, such as math.

Only an unbalanced reality is ever possible for living beings to exist in, and any existences, including ours as human beings, are entirely involved, interwoven, and dependent on mutually creating new environments out of unbalanced opposites.

The nature of such unavoidable change makes us face ever new and different *limitations*. Protagoras' writing was destroyed by the ignorant rulers of his time along with his life, leaving only a few original notes. These notes have been mentioned in Plato's critical writing toward concepts of Flux and limitations ever transforming the world, as these powerful notions destroy his famous *fixed forever ideals*. However, Heraclitus' Flux and Protagoras' Limitations intrigued thinking minds to this day.

In accordance with Protagoras' outstanding and vital ideas, we may extrapolate his thoughts and observe that even a very young child feels, just like adults ourselves, that everything sensed is somehow more or less *limited*, like everything we interact with. This reveals *resistance* of all types, that we sense physically and mentally. Even when some resistance remains invisible, we feel that we "touch" something, or what we may feel as some "tangible object" that somehow more or less resists us. However, the sensation of resistance implies *limitations*.

Limitations frame our ephemeral, uniquely singular experience, which means that the productions of the mind are shaped by limitations within our personal characteristics.

Only through *limitations* are we able to produce sensations, feelings, memories, and thoughts and pursue related activities and deeds of all kinds. The lack of limitations means we become nothing.

Our sensations that we feel as resistance and our experiences of them identify emerging varieties of obstacles of all sorts. Whether painful, joyful, or anything in between, we cannot sense anything without mutual resistance toward what we are already interacting with.

We reside in the existence of opposites and resistance of different natures. Going through potentially endless transformations of Flux, everything is limited simply in order to exist as itself, while being more or less unbalanced to allow new changes to continue.

I would suggest that we observe our limitations not merely as hindrances but as nature's gifts, obstacles that we do not need to always fight but can comprehend and creatively apply to our current reality by changing our behavior and old habits and finding beneficial conditions, mainly internally within our bodies and minds, as the most intuitive living beings do in nature. Nature's *limitations* or resistances, which we endlessly face, mainly serve as our *protective boundaries* that guard us against possible destruction that we are unaware of.

Nature's limitations are like a sculptor's chisel carving us—as living characters of human beings, as well as everything else that exists —out of the infinite metamorphoses of the world.

By continuing to evolve within our myriad limitations this work is endless and vividly inspirational in its nature, the essence of the nature's art of life.

Within our ever-differing circumstances, we are never the same, proving how tremendous the creativity of life is. Life is forever surprising us with new turns, even though it might seem to us the same. Our descriptions of the variety of sensations, such as resistance or limitations, have the following effect on us: activating attraction or magnetic-like compositions of our sensations into experiences from playful opposites, as pointed out by Heraclitus. These sensations would not be able to create our realities without our minds, and their life-producing inborn ability to constantly *compare, select, focus, compose, and recompose* these sensations. Whether poor or immensely rich, life is continuous creativity.

As we use certain devices to augment our extremely underdeveloped bodily organs, we collect increasingly detailed visions of our previous visions and, ironically, reprocess them through the same initially undeveloped corporeal sensory organs. Technologies are limited to serving our physical sensory organs. These technologies only act as our artificial crutches to "explore the world," which do not take us any farther from our human body and still millennia-old basic bodily or physical experience.

Endless forms of life do not perceive what we observe as our visible reality, and obviously do not see us, humans, as something important. For instance, we can see, touch, and measure a wooden desk, but some different forms of life, such as bacteria or viruses, do not even perceive it as a desk, not to mention our own human presence. These tiny beings face no obstacles in passing right through the desk, ignoring its shape, color, texture, and smell, as these characteristics do not exist in their reality. The desk is not "material" either for tiny bacteria or for the world. The desk's "solid" composition is what we sense through our perception that literally creates physical feelings and related visions of what we sense as the desk.

The laws of physics that we learn in schools and deal within our mundane lives are not universal in a world of endlessly unique existences. These laws we study in physics do not exist in the metamorphic Flux. The colossal powers of universal nature are overlooked in our education entirely because these laws initially are not recognized as "physical." We pay attention to what we uniquely sense through our human bodies. However, I would be grateful if my childhood teachers had been able to explain to me that the physical laws we describe and apply in our lives only manifest very limited and specific human conditions of what we call physical or bodily experience. In the worlds of Flux, myriad living organisms have no need for anything such as observations of the planet Earth, Sun, and stars within the "system" of the universe. Different living beings sense the world in myriad interpretations that we would never know.

Bodies are combinations of ephemeral forms of life-producing energy that comprise fields of interactive sensations in the mind. Perhaps what we understand as magnetic fields, as articulated by the great Michael Faraday, are not independent forces external to our minds. Perhaps what we perceive as the cosmos is the result of our minds creating spectacles and impressions processed from our sensations that obviously would not be possible to observe outside our minds—the masters of our realities. Perhaps these energies creating magnetic-like fields outside our minds and bodies from which we may interact, sense, and produce within our internal process of perception are *the opposites*—changes rejecting, attracting, and uniting powers.

It seems that Heraclitus's description of instances of *Flux*, always ignited by the energies of *the opposites*, might point to what we sense and experience as electric fields. The functions of electric currents in contemporary technology–producing electric energy that affects our everyday lives–are what we all experience as they are processed through our fascinating perceptions.

Surviving and evolving uniquely within the colossal powers of the world, the human mind struggles to find the self in the world unobservable to it. While striving to prolong our existence every moment, we must step into new rivers of worlds that are different to us—not just one world, but many.

The human consciousness of "tangible" appearances cannot reflect these myriad worlds. One's reality where one may feel most comfortable as the self is one's authentic sovereign home.

How can we express and share our visions of our own mind? The first artist, a "caveman," demonstrated this by discovering that he could depict some lines and contouring images of visibly familiar shapes on the flattish area on the walls of his cave. A caveman primitively outlined images from his memories that defined the edges of their form. These lines were among the first drawings in human history, a type of art familiar to us as two-dimensional depictions of three-dimensional objects or scenes.

The lines drawn by such early artists somehow became recognizable to our perceptions today, as we have the same "mechanism" of perception as we had millions of years ago. The cave art and the lines depicted on the cave walls were perceived by the rest of the cave artist's tribe or family as something familiar, resembling similar experiences rendered in memories. This tells us that some sketchy images of symbolic lines on a wall have provoked other human minds, while using similar human physical sensory organs, to recognize some shapes by even projecting these simple line drawings and animating them as living characters in each of their own minds. By projecting crude lines onto the imagination and into active stories related to the onlooker's experience, we may share the most fascinating exchange of visions and thoughts. This primordial art reveals a mental process in our instinctive mind, very similar to how we use manmade visible symbols in languages and, beginning later, groups of signs in mathematics and the compositions of symbols in the sciences. The human mental process of perception is always at the inner root of communication and learning.

We still prefer flat surfaces for depicting impressions using paper, canvas, photos, screens, maps, and other surfaces for writing, reading, and illustrating. Our habit of collecting impressions on surfaces leads us to conclusions about the existence of curious spaces, distances, and perspectives that are absolutely impossible within the nature of Flux, as timeless and spaceless instants of Flux have no true time, distances, and therefore no space. We build these temporary conditions in our imagination of sensations from which we compose the playhouses of consciousness.

To prolong our imaginable ephemeral impressions, at least for a while, we instinctively or intentionally find ways to construct and reconstruct similar images in multiple positions, building "perspective" views for these images. However, we can do so only in superficial theatrical and ephemeral consciousness. Perspective, as we further understand, means the imaginative composition of images in the dimensional "stability" of space, which is impossible according to the forever unstable nature of Flux. **Nature's mechanism of perceptions** of the mind plays not only a crucially important role in our entire existence but is also the primary artistic source of our amusing fantasies or productions of what we eventually build to share with others. We call some forms of these expressions "entertainment."

While composing visions, our minds "framing" them into groups of images, similar to framed art pieces. In order to animate the images in them we run them similarly to how we are *animating these images* in a movie. Henri Bergson intuitively discovered the similarity between the effect of the duration we see in movies and our perceiving minds creating visible continuity of constantly fluctuating images. This major development of Henri Bergson in understanding human perceptions of movement has not been truly understood; rather, he received the Nobel Prize for Literature in 1927 for his work *Creative Evolution*.

The wonder of perceiving is a deeply instinctive process of life happening behind the thick mental curtains of the theater of our consciousness. However, it is not difficult to watch how our minds instinctively process fleeting mental impressions into effects of duration, which creates depths of distance by changing related impressions that we try to connect and run through this movie-like rolling-frames mental process.

Later, we will explore how we calculate the speed of light as an "objective" phenomenon while entirely missing the mental process of our own perceiving. The speed of light we perceive is revealing our own limited human speed of perceptions. The speed of light we may measure reveals only the speed of our own corporeal sight. The human perception of physical sight is the most elusive, slippery, and misleading corporeal sensory perception we possess. Merleau-Ponty has been one of the Western philosophers most intrigued by the body as a medium of the primary physical site and the source for our "knowing the world." Since the time of Descartes and Locke, who struggled to comprehend the nature of what we believe consciousness may be and whether it is the only way for us to exist in the world, we, right now, may use different methods to approach the most profound experience of knowing, however, when we respect and learn from the fundamental conditions of Flux.

Remarkably, in his fundamental work *Phenomenology of Perception,* Maurice *Merleau-Ponty* mercilessly exposed and proved the instability and deceptiveness of what we actually *see* based on our perceptions through physical organs.

All questions on perception remain most intriguing in what is called continental as well as in analytical philosophy, still missing the presence of our own minds in all our possible observations. Moreover, this gap in knowledge concerning the fact that our perceptions are never fixed and cannot truly express reality as something exact or perfect leaves professional researchers confused.

From Heisenberg's revelation of the observer effect, we learn the impossibility of observing anything "objectively." Moreover, no one is able to observe anything without affecting and disturbing the objects of one's observations. However, in common thought and specifically in physics and the rest of the sciences, this grand basic knowledge toward our observations has been twisted for the convenience of the previously established idea blindly relying on nonexistent "objectivity."

From the researchers in labs and in the fields of experiments to the average public who easily adopts popular sketchy opinions, the majority are still unable to admit the absolute impossibility of our "objectivity." The ignorance of this sort commonly provokes researchers, scholars, or authorities at all levels and in all fields to be very sure of their own "calculated objectiveness." Moreover, this false confidence is directly related to our human tragedy rooted in our continuous ignorance in general knowledge blindly leading us to myriad small and eventually catastrophic mistakes.

The *observer* effect explains the disturbance of an observed system by the act of *observation.* This crucial knowledge is beyond our basic understanding of our limitations and the functions of our personal and unique sensory perceptions, without which no knowledge can exist at all. Perceptions are possible and functional only with the unavoidable act of momentary interactions.

The lack of awareness among ignorant people who are teaching, governing, and even enforcing mindlessly blind conclusions also makes them unaware of their violating others. Moreover, when interfering in the lives of other unique living beings, these "authorities" in all fields ignore the factual presence of themselves while often acting as uninvited mind-blind intruders.

Heraclitus once mentioned in his notes that the world is "all in one," meaning that it is entirely interactive, with no actual distances inter-effective. However, the world is an endless myriad of interacting worlds, not just one, unless we believe in a man-made "solid" model in our imagination.

Is it possible to "objectively" measure the very speed of some light "out there?" No. Can we at least approximately measure our own human perception as the observer? Yes. According to our human perception of sight, the speed of light in a vacuum, commonly adopted as "a universal physical" constant, is "exactly equal" to 299,792,458 m/s. This statement is commonly understood incorrectly as being based on our ever-interactive human sensations through our relations with the entire world.

An imaginative idea and still naive belief that one appears as "a measure of all things" based on the privilege of being a human being, is only sarcastically expressed by the ancient philosopher Protagoras, the classical teacher on the immeasurable *unavoidable limitations* within the conditions of Flux where we exist. This form of "exact measuring" is only revealing how a "knowledgeable" man can become a grotesque of his pride of ignorance.

Is there "objectivity" in our measurements? However, if the sun is so "far away," why does our skin burn so easily?

When the world "wholeness" implies as "a fixed wholeness" within the powers of instant and continuous change, where nothing may truly be perfectly fixed or balanced, we shall begin our learning from within our own minds.

In any case, we are not born with blank minds. We as living beings are granted the faculty to sense our realities, whether we learn or just fantasize.

To begin to observe our own mind's deeply intuitive and vital *process of perceiving* based on our instant and unstoppable interactions within and without is a grand invitation to take a small step into a breathtaking future of fundamental findings about the nature of ourselves, similar to all living beings we may perceive.

Whether we punish ourselves with poor, boring, and monotonous, or even ugly mental productions, or we work happily to find creative ways to build and master peaceful and harmonious compositions to live in, both "physical," and mental, we have the freedom to choose our ways. However, *there is no true FREEDOM of any sort without RESPONSIBILITY.* **Freedom minus Responsibility equals Madness**.

Thus, we can explore our perceptions in unprecedented ways. Revealing our primordial mind's art, sound recordings, and animation studios, all in one living ephemeral chamber of the mind, we learn about our existence firsthand.

Creativity is rooted in every form of life for the sake of its own life and the continuity of its unrepeatable unique realities.

The continuity of *Comparison* is *our true cure* for the infectious idealism of "objectivity."

Histories of philosophy and the sciences sometimes mention perceptions without even showing any curiosity about *why* we must perceive and *how*. Therefore, our understanding of *the process* of constantly perceiving living minds is limited. To "explain" our visions that we may somehow observe, the majority prefer to refer to medical records and descriptions of bodily organs. Ironically, our physical organs are unable to see, hear, or sense anything on their own. As long as the mind perceives, it is the one who perceives its temporary body.

Now, if we understand that the basic functions of perception cannot be felt directly from sensory organs on their own (still primitively described in medical records and imaging), we would begin to break through the thick walls within established habits of thinking.

"ON BLESSED BLINDNESS,"
by V. Nova

… but if blindness of illusions
disappeared and everyone
could see
Every mind's Kingdom as is,
Feel every feeling and know every thought as one,
Misunderstandings could melt down forever.
Seeds of doubt and blame of others
could stop growing. No fights, wars,
intrigues, hate, no players or
pretending. Alas, no illusions of
beauty, seductive unknowns, or
guesses.
No wonder and no wisdom—
all truths are clear for each mind and for all.

No thrill to admire, no one to thank,
No need to explain, to talk, to act, to scream.
No artist to paint.
No poet to sing.

If my peculiar human senses
cannot give me the world,
God bless my blindness,
the soil for my garden of dreams.
How little I can see with my eyes!
How endlessly I can see and create without them!

God bless my lonely mind in its
sacred solitude, and my only way
To know your world,
By building my own.

CHAPTER TWO

Mathematics and a Young Artist's Still Life: Lessons Beyond School, or 1+1=1

Why Nature does not need mathematics and makes no mistakes

From my very early childhood, those very first impressions of my new reality enchanted me yet also deeply bewildered me, igniting the endless curiosity that remains with me to this day. The questions that children ask come from the perspective of newcomers and independent outsiders who have not yet become entirely involved in the struggle to fit into society and its conventions. As comical as these questions may seem to an adult, the essence of deeply intuitive wonder remains the most precious quality of our nature if we are lucky enough not to suppress it entirely with age.

In a minute or two, my reader will be able to discover a crucial logical mistake in the "exact" sciences, without delving into any specific knowledge in mathematics on which the sciences commonly base their ideas and proof of their accuracy. To our knowledge, this mistake remains the presumable foundation of a very shaky structure of mathematics and an artificial logic ruling our popular mentality that obeys order in our knowledge. Let us consider how easily a young child can detect this broken logic in math when they are beginning to practice it.

In my memories, I return to my earlier days very often, particularly my first impressions of life, which shocked me then. The deepest clarity we may easily experience happens in our early life, before we are taught that we need to be given some generic name and number as our "identity." We are taught that all things must be given names to "know them." Our society demands that artificial IDs be glued to us even before we are born, then we are trained to speak and mimic how other people act to fit in an artificially organized society as well as to communicate using symbolic human language. While receiving such an education and training, I felt that the very unpretentious entity of my self was growing overwhelmed by the ridiculousness of common human behavior and thinking; I was not given any other choice but to accept the established rules.

Human logic reminds me of a tiny fish that swims inside a small bowl, where it is trapped in limited conditions in every direction. Every time the little fish-logic seeks to move forward, it confronts the thick walls of its small chamber. This logic is about facing limitations that we commonly use as a form of guidance and to "know" what to do. This guidance is only possible to apply when it is limited within repetitive or special conditions, measured in terms of "space and time." Otherwise, the fish logic will escape and be lost in the great ocean of nature's endless transformations.

We are about to explore the answer to why, in the first place, our minds are not at all equipped for perfect or objective thinking, and why we cannot completely depend on what seems logical to us, as this is not logical in the world of unpredictable in our mentalities instants of Flux.

Since our school education we are "learning" how to use our man-made (artificially structured) systems of symbols of language and math calculations. One is missing the deeply instinctive, primary natural behavior stemming from the inborn mental abilities of a very young child who is not familiar with a man-made order.

While we are just receiving training in math, we might begin to believe that numbers can grow on trees under their natural conditions.

My earliest impressions remain incomparable; still today, these memories occasionally immerse my life in brilliant light from the past, and I feel as if I am awakening from the dull sleep that we call our "daily life routine." Many of us call this sleep "reality."

I was in the first grade of an ordinary elementary school when my teacher, a relatively older educator, compelled us to memorize 1+1=2. However, this created a conflict with my child's mind. If we take *the very same* imaginatively perfect and ideal 1 and enter it twice, it will remain absolutely *the same 1*. Therefore, intuitive logic indicates that 1+1=1, the same unchanged 1.

To produce a sum—say of two units—the units, or any things being added, must somehow be different. If they are not different, we would perceive them as the same 1 unit or the very same thing. If the units are perfectly the same, they merge as one to be perfectly identical, and they must occupy only one place to have the very same identical conditions and qualities. If these units were identical, we would not be able to differentiate them as many; they would merge into one perfect unit. If we wish for the units that we deal with to become identical, as we are trained to think in math, they would not be able to stay unchanged in any reality of ever-changing environments, but only in our imagination ruled by Plato's "perfect ideals." Ideals would not be able to exist in different places as identical units, not even for an instant, as the real conditions of the mighty Flux would change them instantly and entirely. We agreeably pretend that we see identical units rather than admit that these are only *similar* units or things, and we intuitively approximate them as "the same" units or things. In our early education, we would need to be introduced to the importance of what we understand as *approximation*.

This ability while we are perceiving to *approximate* different appearances as "the same" goes mainly unnoticed in our everyday life as well as in math. In our knowledge of the most colossal natural law of *Flux*, we must admit that any "exact appearances" of anything are impossible. To see "the same" means we depend on the *crudeness* of our perception just in order to *approximate* and imagine "sameness" or even "exactness."

To perceive things, we must *differentiate* between the appearances of things, whether we see them as one or many. To perceive, we must *compare*. To compare, we shall notice some differences in what we are looking at. As we interact within ever-changing conditions, we discriminate between different objects, events, numbers, or whatever we may compare; otherwise, we are unable to perceive anything.

A very young child does not need to become a great philosopher to intuitively discover serious confusion in the well-established concepts that control society and contemporary education. In our early years, we were restricted to thinking in our own ways. From that point on, it is easier for society to begin controlling our early questions with ready-made answers.

That day in my first math class, I sat at my small desk in my elementary school, absolutely bewildered, my little body trembling as I rose, daring to ask my teacher a very silly question in front of my classmates.

"Can the first 1 be bigger or smaller than the following 1s? Or are those 1s absolutely the same units?"

"Certainly, they are the same units—this is math! One apple plus another apple equals two apples. We deal with numbers here!"

I was quiet for a moment, even more bewildered.

"But I do not understand how things like apples can be turned into identical numbers."

My classmates were quiet at first, and then started to giggle.

However, I was not the only child in the world confused by mathematical logic. I thought, "People are so serious about mathematics; they must possess a deeper understanding of what they do. I am not told why … or maybe they just have extraordinary sight and imagination that I do not have. Perhaps they have some supervision when they see the same things, units, and numbers that exist beyond my reality?"

Perhaps my teacher wanted me to pretend that in some extraordinary ideal world of math, the same identical units could really exist unchanged and untouched in different places and times, and independently survive the world of instant change; mathematics can then stay absolutely fixed and unchanged for as long as we wish. Why should she not say this?

Further, in this game in the ideal wonderland of mathematics, those perfect units can be devoured by monsters such as 2, 3, 4, 5, and so on, in such a way that they have a magical ability to reappear, popping back up in their original position, perfectly unchanged, undamaged, and ideal.

Natural science did not seem at all natural to me. In my experiences dealing with reality, things changed mercilessly, never staying fixed or remaining the very same. However, people assign the same conventional symbols to objects such as the sun, a house, a face, a thought, human beings, and other species, all retaining the same designation even when they drastically change their colors, contours, sizes, shapes, behaviors, and movements. Do people play these games on purpose, or do they just not care to truly know much of the essence of anything, but simply categorize and label the misunderstood? In either case, why?

As a young child, I struggled with the curious tasks and explanations given in school, as each of them always had *only one* answer or solution—the "right one." In my mind, I tried to think that if I take one apple once, it will be one time. If I take it twice, it will be two times. Then again, what is "two times"? Are they different or ideal repetitions? In that case, in our reality no matter how many times ideals can be ideally repeated, neither the values nor situations change.

However, in my reality, only crudely perceived "repetitions" would work for mathematical logic. On a little break after that math class I mentioned a moment ago, I conducted my first scientific experiment. I wanted to see if I could calculate repetitive motions. When no one was around, I went downstairs to the rear entrance of my school. I opened the heavy old door with great effort and let it shut by itself. I tried to repeat this procedure a few times in the same way. The door shut each time with a loud groan, but never in exactly the same way as I had expected.

I imagined that this huge old door would eventually fall apart after many movements. A door, like any human machine, moves in *similar* ways, never in *exact* ways, and will do so until it breaks. However, is there any special type of machine that can duplicate exact movements that are absolutely the same? Is there any mechanical clock that ticks so perfectly that it does not need to be rewound?

The answers I was looking for were revealed to me not in my math class, but in my art class. One day, I had to discover and learn about my mind's intuitive behavior when our art teacher introduced my class to a simple method, a common technique intended to help us depict visual images on paper or canvas "proportionally realistic" as a composition. A display for painting my still life was adjusted on top of a small table directly in front of me. My teacher showed me how a pencil could be used to measure these objects and their details at a distance from where I was sitting. While looking at these things, I had to hold the pencil as still as possible, parallel to the object I wanted to measure from this distance. In this manner, I was able to determine how much the length of each displayed object was based on the different portions of the pencil length from the distance where I was. By holding the particular spots on the pencil itself as a scale of my art tool, I could measure different lengths of the subjects while comparing their lengths from the distance. I had to do this repeatedly, looking at all the different objects displayed on the table and using the length of the same pencil to compare all measurements from this distance. I realized that one visible side of a displayed vase would seem longer than another, shorter, more rounded, or oval-shaped, and how much shorter a pear's height appeared compared to the vase's. I was supposed to use these approximated measurements in my painting, using a pencil as a primordial tool that was based on a similar concept in our distance measurements in all sorts.

That traditional "artistic" measuring process amused me as soon as I compared it to a common measuring process in math. A unit can be a pencil in painting a still life or the number 1 in math. This method and the principle of measuring with a pencil in art constitute a process mentally similar to how astronomers measure celestial bodies and the distances related to them, even though their measuring instruments can be highly sophisticated. In both cases, our measurements and calculations depend on the position of the observer, the distance, and the angle from which the subjects were observed. Then again, as we make these calculations, we are missing millions of other factors and events that slip through an abyss beyond our limited corporeal sensory perception. The process of *approximation* in our observations is unavoidable in all our calculations.

Why are our visions so crude even in the pretentiously "exact" structures and orders of mathematics? Can we transcend that crudeness to perfect measurements? These questions appear to be misleading.

Human sight, with its unavoidable limitations, produces the *Crudeness of our visions.* Are we handicapped in perceiving?

One wonders further and may discover for oneself how this very *crudeness* of our perceptions provokes not just deficiency, mistakes, and subsequent pain, but also an impressive creative ability in us. This is the ability of *recognition.*

By skipping endless conditions and details, we create *approximations* of what we are able to observe, and commonly believe that we deal with *"exact" results,* repetitions, answers, or symbols as we still observe them to this day in everyday routine, mathematical, scientific, economic, social, and even religious thinking and reckoning. Our *approximations,* in what we perceive as we *compare,* are unavoidable and more or less good enough for us to assemble what we see and work on into *recognizable* appearances of all sorts.

I came to realize that we instinctively skip a considerable number of real details along with their unstoppably changeable conditions, whether we deal with life, math, or art, so that we do not have to burden ourselves by *comparing* endlessly fluctuating events that are impossible for us to observe for an instant, firmly, or to pause for our inspection. "Climate change" is an unstoppable universal process of unstoppably rotating Earth when an intelligently creative life on our planet evolves and survives. Life exists and thrives intelligently within natural transformations through taking challenges that encouraging creative life to continue, not by following lifeless man-made ideas, models, and activities.

We use abstract, symbolic images to imaginatively fix the wobbly reality of our consciousness to stabilize and adjust its nature to some *collective, approximate impressions and ideas*; hopefully, by doing so, we will become aware of all that. In any case, whether we comprehend this or not, we cannot avoid instant changes within and without ourselves under the universal laws of the magnificent Flux.

In my teen years, since I "analyzed" the functions of an artist's pencil as a primitive measuring tool mimicking our calculations, I recognized that this observation was a major finding for me. We are all capable of depicting our mental impressions as categories, groups, and symbols and models of some sort based on collective and presumably ideal approximations.

This is the fantastic ability we all possess that revealed itself in my art class. With it, we can see how "abstract" arts enable us to reduce details of common impressions to symbols. In math, we see a collection of units, numbers, and symbols expressed as a formula or equation; in classical art, we see it as a still life.

Created by an observer, the composition of abstracted symbols can satisfy our sense of experience, which is forever limited, and therefore incomplete.

Our talent for creating *compositions* even from abstract symbols helps us engage in "framed" thinking, where our logic is locked within limitations/frames set up by us.

However, in the reality of Flux, our thinking is always an abrupt process, which can be compared with walking on crutches from one point to another, constantly missing the conditions and events in between.

We struggle to follow our collective ideas when we deal with very large groups; each of our minds can produce only its own unique, personal version of a "collective" idea. The perfect collective vision, belief, or idea remains our hopeless fantasy, as it is unavoidably based on the comparison and approximation of visible images as some groups, which we label after all as groups of the "same units."

One apple would not be changed by the human "+" symbol, as it exists within its more or less but always unique circumstances and conditions. Apples change their quality and cease to exist as single apples if they are ground together.

We, human beings, get very excited about moving fast at great speeds, and as we fly in a speedy jet from one place to another, we find ourselves totally ignorant of what has been happening in between our departure and destination—how many endlessly invisible, untouchable, yet often fascinating events we have totally missed. We love to jump from one place to another, faster and faster, while flying in a jet or a spaceship, though in the end, we are left amazed, however, having no clue about what has been deeply missing around us.

In my math class, I began to realize that our human minds try to get somewhere without overwhelming themselves by noticing and learning about all the changes and transformations of the world of reality, which remains mysterious to us.

Our experiences in life from the arts, sciences, technologies, and many other established activities in our society are based on the ability to limit everything we perceive by selecting random impressions on which we decide to work and skipping the rest. This is our knowledge as we trust it today. This method of thinking is routinely applied in the sciences, mathematics, and philosophy and is known as reductionism.

One extraordinary day, I was overwhelmed by discovering the great ancient Greek philosopher Heraclitus, who depicted *Flux*, the unavoidable condition of the world. A very young child can potentially be a great philosopher since a child can recognize sensations of Flux. We cannot escape Flux anywhere. The world's continuously changing nature is the only condition of fundamental constancy.

"No man ever steps in the same river twice, for it's not the same river and he's not the same man" — through this assertion, Heraclitus explained what Flux is over two and a half millennia ago. I did not need to be convinced—I already knew that my own self could not stay the same self even for a moment. I am always entirely different, constantly swimming in an ocean of wonder of transformations.

Mathematics is simply trying to stand unchangeably stagnant in a river of Flux in which one cannot step twice.

While this is hard to admit, we function and think within mathematical rules only with approximations that are more or less realistic for us. However, it seems to mathematicians that they can fight and even correct the fundamental law of Flux just *based on our misleading human imagination regarding our possibilities of "reflections" of realities when "controlled" under man-made rules.* Things and numbers therein are fixed in every position and combination according to a stubborn mathematician. When the same labels are glued onto different things, they can present the same numbers, reducing the real characteristics of the objects to mere labels and units. Do they? Things in the wonderland of mathematics can also conveniently remain unchanged to allow someone time to consider what to do with them. In reality, this is impossible because of the mighty Flux of the world.

As a common practice in daily life and the sciences, we limit and cage the subjects of our contemplation to simplify our vision and thinking. We frame it as we frame our artwork while cutting off some visible but curiously related appearances to avoid complications and struggle to understand the chosen subjects without much insight into the details associated with them. Consequently, we make incomplete calculations, unaware of making small and catastrophic errors.

However, we trust our calculations and statistics to judge our circumstances and environments of all types. This is understandable, as we still have extremely underdeveloped sensory perceptions and intuition. Although it is crucial to acknowledge that all our calculations and measurements are approximations, they are still helpful in compensating for the crudeness of our observations and comprehension of what we may see.

While summarizing events, especially in great numbers, based on recorded appearances and visions, we can construct crude models by simplifying our complicated environments.

Our calculus cannot be objective, as it entails summarizing incomplete and random information. The information changes faster than our deductions, and we are prone to drawing misleading conclusions of all sorts. Check and recheck what you see and think it over based on constant *comparison*.

People who do not learn much on their own but catch soundbites from popularized twisted "scientific" ideas from the media are prone to panic and confusion. Meanwhile, only a few researchers have been devoted to extremely thorough work, collecting records on developments across different subjects and events, sometimes since the dawn of our history.

Those who struggle to "fix" nature instead of developing our own abilities to evolve ourselves within ever-changing nature's turns, "create" no solutions but various "fixing" disasters within the local and especially global environment, which are irreversible. Most alarming is the "global change" joints of individuals continuously advertising ill-conceived ideas and activities over global "control" based on curiously twisted, incomplete, and patched statistics derived from highly irresponsible research. The naïve and scared populations are donating millions and even billions to these activities "fighting" changing for billions of years climate that they cannot comprehend. We punish ourselves and the rest of the life on our planet because of our own collective ignorance, bringing great destruction to our planet. Since its birth, Earth has been the largest producer of CO_2. Human production remains minuscule and sometimes even below 5% of that of nature. Moreover, life on Earth and its ecosystems—forests, plants, and oceans—would not last without CO_2.

Media statistics are often purposely incorrect and also pushed forward as "information" (which could be considered abusive) to control naïve masses and convince them to accept sinful activities such as geoengineering.

Statistics can trick, mislead, and ultimately abuse our imagination in every field of experience. Our knowledge of Earth's climatic changes remains limited at a nascent stage.

However, as long as we are still greatly limited in our knowledge, some carefully checked and rechecked statistics can be very helpful despite the unavoidable crudity and errors of any sorts of our computing. The best results require a significant effort in constant corrections based on all possible comparisons.

One day, one might watch a thousand people marching down the streets shouting about their one "shared idea." These people wholeheartedly believe that they follow the same idea and expect the same results from their actions. In actuality, they are not one solid group numbering one million but groups of different individual minds and bodies who only wish to be recognized as if they are one entity. Although their minds and bodies may interact intimately, they are not a single unit or idea. As soon as people with "one idea" get more closely acquainted, they feel shocked to see how different every one of them is, as well as how their "same idea" appears almost unrecognizable within each different mind expressing itself. Therefore, all movements of large crowds are sooner or later doomed to fall apart.

Whether we observe complicated microscopic appearances or large spectacles such as cosmic events or crowds of people, we want to see systematic and "framed" order. Our tendency to take control of complicated events that we never can truly understand or know somehow stimulates us to build inflexible and oversimplified "robotic" systems, as we now see with our prevailing artificial societal systems. The larger the systems we build, the more uncontrollable they become, eventually falling apart and becoming impossible to fix. In spite of the impossible ideal "machines" to organize, equalize and control our existence, ironically, these systems are unavoidably self-destructive creating both environmental and economic catastrophes. Therefore, smaller systems of all possible varieties are easier to build, maintain, and adjust, and when they fall apart with time, these smaller varieties do not inflict devastating disasters upon the planet as the huge ones do. Small systems are much easier to be replaced with better ones.

Sooner or later, people who have believed in "the same idea" for all would be forced to admit that the concept of the "same idea" is the product of our imagination. Only small groups of individuals, when interactive, can soberly come to mutually agree on ideas by exchanging thoughts and experiences through peaceful and productive collaboration. This allows our existence to constitute both peaceful and exciting moments, based on exchanging life experiences with myriad creative skills, productions, and workable plans.

Nature has none of the ideal machines or unchanged stable structures that we dream about. Uniqueness is in the core of life.

Although our presumably exact repetitions in systems are impossible in nature, mathematics serves as a splendid example of how we try to manage to mistakenly put different things into the same groups, equations, and various calculations and isolate these groups and systems from the rest of the world.

The law of physics shall reveal the basic natural conditions in our existence. However, we are still missing in our thinking the fundamental knowledge on nature from which we are "made of." We cannot completely isolate our models from the endless and ever-new turns of nature's which we fail to notice through its entire net of interactive forces.

In ancient times, arithmetic was invented to help people in trade, because "things" and animals are impossible to estimate exactly in their varieties of values. You can buy a few camels for a piece of silver or gold. Money conveniently allowed people to adhere to trade rules and was adopted in Egypt. Arithmetic was successfully practiced in Egypt for a long time before it was learned in Greece, again, first through trade. The Greek philosophers then began creating and putting in order simple numerical symbols and developing philosophical theories of mathematics, later introducing established mathematical logic as systems of balancing "perfect" units as numbers and symbols in groups.

As a child, I wondered why it is that in our postmodern society, everything must be calculated as numbers—houses, cars, money, fingers, people, animals, stars, or pages of a book. A bird flies to its destination without the need for maps, directions, watches, or artificial fuel; any wild animal finds its sources of food and safety—it jumps mostly perfectly to an accessible point and catches what it needs, and it can sense changes in weather before our contemporary technology can. Animals develop their own protective fur, shells, or scales that keep them comfortable and safe even despite the "climate changes" and predators of their environments.

We do not develop our own bodily perceptions of our sensations and abilities to adapt to nature but prefer to invent our artificial languages of symbolic ideas, words, or measurements as numbers, as we wish to control everything we can reach by twisting and adjust everything to our endless needs in the way we want to imagine our reality. When we must face nature's sudden turns, some of us eventually come to realize how dysfunctional our life is, with most of our conveniences based on artificial communications, conditions, "artificial intelligence" (AI), and production of energy.

We are very misled by the illusions of being superior to the rest of nature when, in reality, our thinking and deeds only prove that our tricky ways of trying to get what we want soon cause harm. This harm eventually returns to us as a dangerous boomerang. Nature has absolutely no need to speak our languages but is in constant interaction, and not even the tiniest human movement or act can be missed without response/reaction. Nature does not need to learn human language, but humans do need to learn nature's messages and signs.

The following chapters present a new perspective that will enable a student, researcher, medical doctor, teacher, or any interested person to view their reality and work in unprecedented ways, suggesting new methods of looking at what seems already known. Many subjects of our existing research cry out for revision and rethinking; this perspective can, therefore, reveal new and unexpected findings. When these discoveries become personal, they may inspire and enhance a person's life forever.

Mathematics is built upon the most "fantastic" logical errors, most of which still go unnoticed, even by such mathematician-logicians as Bertrand Russell or the brilliant Kurt Gödel.

Sometimes, as adults, we recognize our rigid mental patterns in perceiving and acting, calling this a "tradition," or even "knowledge." We are trained to become accustomed to these patterns since childhood, and by the time we have reached adulthood, we hardly distinguish those common behavioral habits from our true life experience. Even people can be manipulated as approximate subjects in the ruling authorities' calculus.

Symbols and signs represent crudely collected and approximated experiences that are shared with or addressed to a person who can decode these signs and presume some of their value. We often refer to this as knowledge.

As mentioned earlier, the sciences urgently need to scrupulously revise their outdated methods of observing and comprehending natural design limited by superficial observations of appearances. As they exist today, the sciences cannot prove or disprove any experience outside of made-up models, systems, categories, and laboratories, all under manmade rules.

When loud cacophonies we "create" are destroying us and we are screaming and losing our own singing voices, the blessed deeply intuitive abilities we are all granted can rescue us, leading us to safety within harmonious survival.

CHAPTER THREE

The Controversial Golden Rule and the Speed of Light, or the Speed of Our Perception

In his superbly intuitive description of our perception of duration and of how we possibly derive visible impressions that we wrongly mistake for an unbreakable flow, Henri Bergson states, "no two moments are identical in a conscious being" (*The Creative Mind*, p. 164). Duration, for Bergson, entails the continuity of progress and heterogeneity; he describes the seemingly flowless duration that we perceive when we depend on our corporeal sight as random impressions in our consciousness. This effect is usually described as "sequence analogies," which may involve comparing events, objects, or actions.

When making measurements, observing what we consider "space" might be, however, is based on the comparison of unique moment-by-moment impressions that our imagination instinctively composes on a flattish stage of consciousness within "flowless" movements of "distances in space." To make us feel some sort of "space," our perceptions produce momentary impressions that seem to move somewhere in the mind's theatrical consciousness. In consciousness, in a part of our mind, we process sensations into compositions of "pictures" or what we call visions, which cannot stop fluctuating as we perceive only unstable, swiftly different appearances of these visions, akin to "frames" in animation productions. We cannot perceive any perfectly stagnant, unchanged appearance. These impressions in our minds are similar to how we observe an appearance in any format, such as photos or painted images in movies, using which are created animation sequences that appear to us as movement. What one observes as a "movement in space" is a *process of the ever-changing perception* one may discover in one's own mind's functioning.

The invention of movies is, after all, not a true invention; rather, it is based on an instinctive discovery of the fantastic internal ability of our minds to create moving sequences while interpreting our momentary sensations, especially those we perceive through the organic transmitters of the brain, eyes, and ears. We can now transmit different sorts of signals based on instinctively mimicking natural mental behavior, but we still cannot comprehend the process clearly explained by H. Bergson in our technological development. We can artificially produce lifeless robotic signals and transmit them onto the flat screens of our TVs or computers, eventually collecting them within the framed compositions of images displayed on the screens of our devices. These human-produced momentary signals or "pixels" are possible for human brains to sense as described in quantum mechanics as radio waves, quarks, particles, or waves. Such inventions, accessible using the sensory perceptions of physical bodies, require scrupulous research involving observations of our mental states and unique primary perceptions affected by the unavoidable, fluctuating conditions of our environment, where we have no actual distances or movements, as we imagine and build our models of physical reality. We do not yet view the effect of distance as a sequence of different transformations allowing no space either within ourselves or anywhere beyond us. This issue cannot be researched, comprehended, or solved within our existing institutions and knowledge systems.

Ernest Mach and Albert Einstein have a history of heated arguments: Mach's positivism initially stood on the idea that if one wants to prove something to us, we must literally see it. The concept of positivism has guided contemporary researchers to this day. However, to "prove" an aspect of nature's terms and conditions, one can only use one's own perceptions (and can do so within oneself only). Heisenberg's *observer effect* remains largely uncomprehended and underappreciated in physics. Distances are what we presume to be proof of our separation from where we may be and the distant objects we observe. When we are already involved in perceiving these objects, we interact with these objects regardless of where and how we see them. We are never truly separated from anything, whether or not we see something. The interactions among the ever-changing events of Flux affect the mighty world entirely, and we are also affected entirely, whether or not we sense the reasons for our own transformations.

As we approach what we observe in space, we keep transforming ourselves, facing an ever-changing environment along the way. I have described above our sense of motion without analyzing the term "space," as it remains a rather obscure feeling and it has never been possible to prove as the objective existing condition of the world. The terms material and matter have been a great subject of heated arguments among philosophers who have commonly been categorized by scholars as materialists or idealists. In all cases, the quintessential task of explaining *how human visions are getting into our minds* in the first place is entirely missing.

The popular teachings of Vladimir Lenin, the widely read Soviet ruler and political organizer, are confusing, revealing his ignorance of classical history. As a pseudo-philosopher, he authored and published numerous books with borrowed ideas, wherein he expressed inexhaustible hatred toward classical philosophers such as Ernest Mach and stood firmly on primitive points of positive constructivism (a term articulated by August Comte, *1798–1857*).

The great Mach defended a profound position in knowledge—the idea that we may only recognize our realities through sensations. Mach adhered to a type of phenomenalism that recognized only sensations (such as our corporeal sight) as real, and after the well-known lecture in 1897 by Ludwig Boltzmann at the Imperial Academy of Science in Vienna, Mach declared that atoms do not exist. His criticism of Newton's position on space and time, which he considered human illusions, influenced Einstein's work.

The most challenging task involves determining *how we sense* at all and putting sensations together in our visions, feelings, thinking, dreams, or imagination, which remain unexplored. I have suggested a few explanations in my notes. This allows us to contemplate the behavior of the mind and the basic vital artistic nature of our own mentalities.

Most recognized works on discoveries within nature face a grand problem: the question of *how* we manage to perceive and what kinds of conditions unavoidably affect our minds and bodies even before we perceive anything at all—this lies ahead of us.

The basic requirement which is a must for a serious researcher is to learn how we exist under the world's fundamental laws of nature, which we sense every instant.

Our knowledge, based on what we see, remains highly questionable, as we create man-made rules and conditions just to prove our findings. (Merleau Ponty's *Phenomenology of Perception* is crucial to read before becoming a physicist, mathematician, teacher, or politician, to learn about the endlessly illusive visions in the theater of what we call consciousness that we mistake for an objective "world's reality").

Can the observer see anything at all objectively? If we think more thoughtfully regarding God to whom we pray as the Creator, would we be able to confidently state that the mighty Creator is endlessly occupied with putting endless confusion, jealousy, envy, anger, cruelty, stupidity, and bloody ignorance into our individual minds to test each of us for goodness and intelligence, while, after all, we have been fantastically and generously granted from birth—like every other living being—wonderful abilities to perceive the world and ourselves in unique ways, and have the blessed freedom and our own responsibility to choose our best ways to act accordingly? With these inborn abilities to sense and perceive the world as we choose, do we learn to create masterfully and harmoniously by following the wisest steps of the Creator? Shall we keep begging the Creator for his forgiveness for our stupidity, laziness to know, and cruelty of ignorance? Or are we willing to learn from Mother Nature's ultimate school all we can comprehend, and even beyond? First, the following fundamental questions have never been answered. *How do we sense and see, hear, or smell in the first place? Why are we granted the faculties to be creative while using these wonderful inborn abilities?* The basic answer is that blessed creativity is born with us *for the sake of continuity of our life, survival, and evolution.* There are no rewards or trades in heaven. Your spirit is given the freedom to choose to create what you deserve.

All that we see, we presumably believe exists somewhere on its own, out there, and we, human beings, just watch all of it using our bodily eyes, our physical organs, for sight. However, it is not "there," as in the first place we cannot look at anything "outside" ourselves directly. We may only see appearances, when they are perceived and processed in our minds, by our minds.

Trying to prove what we see as objectively true is impossible based on our individually limited and unique sensory perceptions.

What helps is to learn to share our more or less unique experience sincerely with others. The fields of physics and chemistry are discovering not universal but these internal life conditions of our perceptions of the human mind and specific sensations from interactions with temporary bodies.

Physics explains the effects while we are receiving initial sensations through our bodily organs, including our brain. However, as previously mentioned, no one can find any image or thought in the brain, which is only an organic transmitter between the body and mind. The human evolution since prehistoric time is still based on bodily human transformations, recorded from on archeological discoveries of the fragments of human fossils, however missing the presence of transformations of living minds responsible for drastically affecting the human corporeal bodies by evolving or degrading them during millions of earthy years.

Scientists or researchers initially receive sensations based on what their minds have perceived from their bodily sensory organs while ignoring the experience of the work of the mind. The work of the mind, putting together visible presentations, makes possible for scientists and researchers to imaginatively stage mental scenarios in their consciousness, while they still believe they observe our "realities of the world."

As we discover within ourselves the way our minds literally perceive and assimilate our primary instant-by-instant sensations following our deeply instinctive internal *mechanism of perceptions*, we are on our way to discovering the world's nature of metamorphosis and its fundamental mighty laws, but only through ourselves, as our existence is inseparable from these vital laws.

The mind is the most fascinating little creator we may ever intimately know. "Every man's world picture is and always remains a construct of his mind and cannot be proved to have any other existence," said Erwin Schrödinger in *Mind and Matter*.

When we try to "fix" and adjust our man-made rules to life, we are already unavoidably affected by *limitations* from different conditions within and without ourselves. No matter how hard we try to control our experience by applying our fixed rules, the universal laws of *limitations affect* our sensations while constantly fluctuating. These *limitations* or obstacles cannot be truly "fixed," even if we perceive and touch them through our corporeal sensory organs and see life as recorded "fixed" photos, screens, or graphic images. It is not possible to perfectly isolate anything within very thick walls of any sorts.

As we read above, we see all impressions instant by instant as "frames" in which we see some images transform in the manner of a "succession without absolute distinction," explains Bergson, which only reveals, I would like to point out here, the *crudeness* of our human sight. There is no true stability in our existence within the magnificent Flux; this is why our mind works in a similar way to an animation workshop, but at first, everything happens in our own ephemeral "animation studio" of the human mastermind.

Ironically, proofs in the sciences are based mainly on recorded appearances perceived through corporeal sight, which are imitations of the gathered impressions of our corporeal sight on flat surfaces. As mentioned, our perception through our corporeal bodily eyes is known in the field of the psychology of human perception as the most deceptive and superficial sensory perception of all those we possess.

The sciences have a great need to thoroughly revise and change their outdated methods of observing and understanding our own nature. In fact, the sciences as they exist today still cannot prove or disprove any experience outside their scientific, highly self-restrictive mentality, which mainly depends on the appearances of recorded visions, categories, and experiences in closed laboratories, all under controlled man-made rules. We are still unaware that our calculations are based on the "identical units" of numbers and symbols impossible in nature, and therefore absolutely cannot reveal any fragment of living reality.

Even when we manage to augment the physical functions of bodily organs with technological devices, we still rely on poor and medically naïve explanations of the same bodily organs and their limited functions, ignoring the unavoidable processing taking place within mind perceptions, as we still cannot explain operations related to perceptions of the mind—not the bodily organs, including the brain, but the mind that perceives.

Such an outdated mentality only makes us more opinionated rather than truly knowledgeable.

Meanwhile, the artificially built technology that we attempt to rely on to enhance our perceptions neither truly proves much about humankind's supposedly great progress nor reveals the evolution of our mental intelligence.

Ironically, whether in the sciences or in our mundane life, we prefer to stay unaware of the disturbing fact that we choose to depend almost entirely on our corporeal sensory perception of sight, which, in multiple research fields as I have mentioned earlier, has been proven to be the most deceiving of all the perceptions we possess. Shall we keep this in mind?

Astonishingly, AI that convinces us that we *desperately need artificial crutches* for what we concede as "progress." However, this notion may help us discover that we are so undeveloped as physical living beings that the salvation we see in building the artificial machines and robotic systems we create appear as systems serving us as our crutches for invalids.

We believe in "progress" while quite obviously demonstrating how very needy and vulnerable we are in almost every way.

While traveling through the cosmos, ultimately, we remain vulnerable bodies trapped inside survival capsules, and these bodies cannot evolve in artificially fixed surroundings. While our bodies are traveling through the cosmos, our minds are going practically nowhere from themselves; instead, we are simply watching mental impressions of the superficial consciousness of the mind as "cosmos" and "ourselves" as bodies in it. It is our mind that senses our bodies, and not vice versa.

When suppressed by rigid human intuition, which restricts our thinking, we must compare ourselves with animals or other forms of life that are deeply intuitive and endlessly innovative under nature's continuous changes and challenges. All living creatures constantly adjust their temporary bodies in deeply creative ways, without needing huge industries to produce clothing, energy, food, or means of transportation.

We are about to learn to explore our blessed creative abilities within ourselves, at least to some degree, beginning with this endlessly pioneering research and inviting the next generation of curious and revolutionary humane practitioners from all fields.

Because living beings are under the mighty laws of the world, we have never truly studied ourselves. We must comprehend our own mistakes that are blindly materialized for the sake of our common and temporary conveniences, as with our unstoppable "advancements" filling up our very thin atmosphere worldwide with all kinds of flying technological gadgets, systems, and man-made materials, depriving us of our naturally designed protective atmosphere; indeed, we are facing disasters for which the entire planet and all other species pay dearly. It is well known that the ozone layer, which protects us from cosmic radiation, is being depleted by human activities, especially such as an ongoing, as we speak, highly polluting the air, water and soil project as "Dimming the Sun." The great responsibility for our man-made activities, based on highly questionable ideas and endless ignorance, is missing.

God's nature gives us all the primary abilities to survive, create, and evolve uniquely however, only under its vital laws.

We have been generously granted all the internal natural "tools" to act entirely as little creators rather than destroyers. For the sake of our own survival, we are here to learn from nature's ultimate school and explain what we do.

The speeds of any of our measurements lag far behind those of the mighty *Flux* of our world. We are late in everything that we may perceive and know. Nevertheless, we are not late for ourselves within ourselves. Whether facing disasters or happy moments, we are "right on time." We are reborn into a new existence of new circumstances and possibilities moment by moment.

You are here to prove the great Werner Heisenberg's teachings on the impossibility of "certainty" is the universal condition. All our attempts to produce "certainty" rely only on what we may randomly sense and process through our moment-by-moment changes within human bodily sensations.

As mentioned above, the greatest physicist and philosopher of our time, Werner Heisenberg, suggested the fundamental understanding of the effect produced by us while we "only" observe some "objects" or events, a concept unheard of before in the sciences. He introduced us to the presence of observers who cause transformative change within whatever they observe. The uncertainty theory is rooted in the universal laws of Flux.

A similar notion based on observations about the world that is interconnected is known in old history as the "butterfly effect," or in the sciences, the "ripple effect." These observations have never been explained.

The basic knowledge on Flux proves that there is no certainty, or that perfect correctness is simply impossible.

This fundamental knowledge is entirely missing from learning in physics, mathematics and chemistry—any existence of any sort is always facing irreversible momentary transformations; therefore, it is never perfectly predictable, calculable, or visible, even as the most minuscule event, because transformations of any existence occur far ahead of our human perceptions and comprehension.

To this day, even sharp minds face difficulties in finding theoretical proofs based on mathematics in an attempt to model our imaginable systems of stability and perfection. We must learn to expect new changes and challenges.

Only a few great minds have desperately tried to find possibilities for engaging what is already known with new findings and new visions to adjust our practical experiences to our methods of thinking. Kurt Gödel is known for his *incompleteness theorems*, which are *two theorems of mathematical logic that are concerned with the limits of provability in formal axiomatic theories*. In any reasonable mathematical system, these theorems hold; there will always be statements that cannot be proven, either within any theory or in real experience, or as a theory referring to a man-made model.

The seventeenth-century German philosopher and mathematician Gottfried Wilhelm Leibniz used his symbolic images of letters to calculate the instantaneous rate of change in order to describe a function of noticeable change graphically, as the slope or curve for visible observations, especially of the *light* rays reflected from concave mirrors. This serves as an innovative approach to observing the phenomenon of light. However, who is the observer and interpreter of these impressions, sifting the impressions of these experiments in their unique mind?

Furthermore, what is light and how do we understand "the speed of light," which presumably lies outside our perceptions? Does it?

As our minds cannot perceive anything without the internal *mechanism of our perceptions*, processing our random primary interactions of different aspects of nature within our mind, can the speed of light reveal outer, universal conditions? Not even close, I argue, but why? Light as we perceive it is a phenomenal condition created within our own human perception—what we human beings sense and recognize as light per our visualization and reasoning is an internal mental process, revealing how we fail to notice that what we sense as light is not universal but the explainable condition produced within a living creative mind.

We eventually sense this light through our bodily organs when our minds interact with our bodies. We commonly trust that we are able to see "reflected" light on the surfaces of different objects, or so it seems.

The speed of light is still based on questionable experiments, such as those done with fast-changing mirrors and those that aim to measure the speed of light in a vacuum, commonly denoted as "c," a universal physical constant that is exactly equal to 299,792,458 m/s. According to the theory of relativity, c is the upper limit for the speed at which conventional matter or energy can travel through space. What kind of energy and what sort of space?

Does a mind produce energies that we sense from within, which we may perceive as light, whether it appears as a candle, flashlight, explosion, lightning, the sun, and stars, or a dream? These impressions in the first place still mysteriously emerge from internal sensations of energy within ourselves and may seem to us as coming directly from universal conditions.

How do we sense light in mental events such as dreams? Is what we sense as light of all sorts our own specific and internal reaction toward our own interactions within environmental conditions that uniquely affect us?

Whether our mind is receiving sensations through corporeal sensory organs such as our eyes, ears, and nose or through ephemeral but powerful mental sensations, we keep transforming ourselves entirely within the ever-changing realities of our existence.

Light is the most fascinating and penetrating form of energy that we may produce, within ourselves. However, light can never indicate the "speed" and qualities of the mighty conditions of Flux. The "speed" of the transformations of the world are incalculable.

We can only try to imagine the possible "speed" of transformations of the magnificent world that remain unknowable to us except through our observable spectacles of mentally composed visions of the internal spectacles of the universe.

We might start developing some fantastic new thoughts and even have great fun playing out our variations of possible events in the world — this time, perhaps based on *different* "speeds of light."

In the past, physicists were not sure that light could have limitations. Einstein suggested that there can be some kind of limit to speed in the universe; however, he proposed this only to carry out specific calculations using his equations, based on the visible-to-the-human-eye cosmic space and measurable "distances." The "speed limit" makes possible for humans to actually see, record, or photograph images of light using our bodily organs, such as our eyes. Einstein's famous calculous was based on limitation of our human perception of what we see as light. (Light, when measured in a vacuum, or a presumably "empty space," does not travel faster than 300,000 km/s or 186,000 mi/s; so is the case with our perception of it). Einstein was an intuitive philosopher and was never sure of any constant speed as a condition in the outer-for-us world. He suggested the symbolic speed of light as a constant ultimate speed for math and physics, which served as a convenient unit with which to balance his equation.

Perhaps the outstanding philosophers of the past have been depicting the existence of the universal powers igniting its endlessness of the mighty world, with "Fire" (light, and heat, burning toward the ends and new beginnings) and "Water" (perhaps symbolizing time and transformation). By revealing these instances, we go through, where no space and time can exist even in our imagination and for any man-made vision of modeling atoms, particles of matter, or quarks, Heraclitus, a pioneer of knowledge of nature, teaches us of *Flux.*

According to this principle, the world of instants has no time for any time and no space for any space.

Nature's mechanism of the mind's perceptions is indispensable and necessary for the sake of the continuity of every living existence.

As our society has so much admiration for ourselves and our intelligence and beauty, especially when "accentuated" with artificial technologies for controlling and fighting against nature because we do not understand its turns, we prefer to observe theatrical "consciousness" as our only source of knowledge. We ignore the fact that all that we see through our corporeal sight is based on illusive impressions that are processed and sifted through our very limited physical organs.

We desperately (and uselessly) seek some ultimate "order" to follow. However, the idea of an order under man-made control would only fight against the natural vitality and metamorphic powers of life. "Dictatorship naturally arises out of democracy and the most aggravated form of tyranny and slavery out of the most extreme liberty," remarked Plato. Curiously, his *Republic* presents a horrific example of social tyranny for the sake of the idea of order. Plato himself carried immense grief after losing his beloved teacher, the great philosopher Socrates, who was forced by the highly ignorant ruling authorities to poison himself in front of his faithful students. However, the problem of tyranny for the sake of "order" is as old as humanity itself, as ignorance based on a lack of basic ethics arises at every turn in our societies, whether tribal or more complex. We commonly fight against noticeable tyranny while exploring another unnoticed and typically bloody form of tyranny: the mindless concentration of power given to those with ignorantly primitive minds, which allows them seemingly unlimited rule. Many believe that man-made violence is beneficial for its ability to "easily" allow rulers to lead and control people without much of soberly thinking. Primitive cases of "control" are always mindlessly abusing trapped individuals as well as the "no-go" weak-minded rulers themselves. From as far back as Aristotle's view on a tyrant who has no public interest whatsoever, an observation we can all agree on, we see that Tyranny has many faces and exists across many levels, but it has no responsibility for its "free" made-up ideas and ends in its mindlessly rotting decomposition. The governments are chosen to *serve people who choose them*, not rule anyone. A great leader is extremely rare as he possesses a sound mind of a great practitioner and a fast learner.

I have never believed that my physical body, which is a composition of different forms of life alien to myself, such as a variety of cells, tissues, bacteria, and viruses, can be my Self. In early childhood, I actually felt scared of my clumsy little body when I noticed a couple of tiny blue veins in my wrist.

I could barely hear my voice, but I felt sure that I knew myself, vigorous form of light itself, communicating everywhere I wished, with no language, using any vessel to travel or voice to speak. I have read about similar experiences of other people who have suffered brief paralysis following brain damage. Not a brain but the very mind sees, hears, feels, and ultimately recognizes it's entity. We are all born with a strong primary awareness of our previous life as bodiless minds, which we often retain throughout early childhood. This fascinating research on what we call the out-of-body experience is a pioneering approach that merits further attention.

In my futuristic comedy of manners, *The Noble Society of Bullford,* the denizens of this playful community lightyears away from our human society, called Bullfordians, have unique identities of living spirits and their own advanced Golden Rule teaching a dictum opposite to Plato's version of Golden Rule, "May I do to others as I would that they should do unto me." Similar sayings have existed since historical times in many cultures and societies, even before Plato. However, Bullfordian wisdom tells us, **"*Never* treat others as you would like to be treated yourself— unless they agree to it first—because what is good for you may be deadly damaging for others."**

Bullfordians have no physical bodies, as they have no need for them. The gift of nature is our ability to exist as unique living individuals, their society understands.

In our world of magnificent Flux, we cannot survive as identical units treated under the same order or force. Henri Bergson once stated in his 1903 essay, *Introduction to Metaphysic*s that no two moments may ever be identical in the consciousness of a living being.

CHAPTER FOUR

Acting Abilities for Life: Come and Meet Your Self

How does a mind, as an entity of the Self, manage to recognize
itself, communicate, and even understand others?

How do we manage to express ourselves to others while remaining
unique as individual and sovereign living beings?

"SILLY SONG," by Federico García Lorca from "A silly song and twelve poems"

Mama,
I wish I were silver.
Son,
You'd be very cold.
Mama,
Embroider me on your pillow.
That yes!
Right away!

The famous Spanish poet Federico García Lorca played everyone and everything in his mind while writing his lovely poem—even his mother's silver and her pillow—while adopting the persona of a young boy in his unique imaginable scenario.

When reading this poem, we imagine a poet who describes himself as a young child speaking to his mother. When one reads this poem, one instinctively plays all the characters in this poem by Lorca on the stage of one's own mind. These stages appear within everyone's mental theater that we call consciousness, where we are simultaneously actors, directors, and observers, depicting ephemeral plays and stories which we fulfill with animated images.

This mental process is absolutely necessary. No matter how tremendously the sensations we experience might affect us—whether pleasant or painful, scary or peacefully comfortable—we cannot imagine anything unless we are creating in our minds the entire theatrical production, including the characters, "things," and their backgrounds, that our minds internally design and act out.

What we call "imagination" serves as our mind's stage where this internal acting of characters and subjects plays out. However, we have no clue about how this miraculous work of the mind is processing the reality we presume is "out there." Is the reality only perceived personally? Or can it be somehow experienced collectively, as if we presume we all see "the same reality," but only in personal minds? If so, why do we unceasingly argue about what we see?

While we are reading, we are playing our roles in our minds, like those of the poet and the poet's mother, to whom the poet is talking as a young boy. Moreover, we may also pretend to be things and imaginative conditions, such as silver, imagining its texture, color, and coldness to the touch. As readers, our minds have to keep animating images for the character we envision, keeping them in motion, while we unavoidably feel our presence "over there" as a personal participant.

Our minds have absolutely remarkable abilities to play as many characters as possible while shaping a range of characters in the ways we imagine them. This is how our perceptions of what we call "objective" reality are processed in our minds.

Whether we are poets or scientists, philosophers or detectives, army commanders or simply commoners reading stories, we absolutely cannot observe, think, or memorize anything without primarily staging our observations in our minds and mentally acting out our thoughts, memories, fantasies, and judgments based on different characters. We produce as many mentally created characters as we may imagine, and whether we intuitively sense them well or poorly or label them as some categories and therefore wrongly judge them, all depends on our inborn acting talents and creativity, which means imitating or mimicking others. We may reveal ourselves as very primitive "bad actors" by judging other living beings or "things" based on our own poor experiences of all sorts. We judge our experiences on the stage of our own consciousness, seeking some possible coherence, where we unavoidably coordinate ourselves as leading characters, whether we comprehend our own presence as such or not. We are mainly opinionated based on what we are able to comprehend and memorize. This uniquely human experience that we observe on our mind's stage as knowledge displays our internal acting abilities as well, and this phenomenon awaits deep study ahead.

Acting like someone we want to resemble and then somehow visualizing this helps when we are trying to predict some character's actions; however, when we are mistaken, this can be a confusing and stressful emotional experience that tragically affects us. To comprehend how our internal acting may affect our entire life, we shall call for our intuition beyond the curtains of our theatrical consciousness.

Once in a while we do not need human communication using words. Animals become extremely emotional when they trust humans, live closely, and in some cases are willing to die with someone they are attached to.

If any animal is able to sense its environment on many different levels, using no human technology and yet sensing far beyond what we humans normally perceive in superficial consciousness, why are we so surprised?

Walker Percy once deliberated on why there is such a gap between humans and nonspeaking animals, presenting his theory on humans as unique "speaking creatures."

We cannot absolutely know "things in themselves," as the great George Berkeley articulates that notion for the first time (Kant only later adopted this Berkeley's thought.) We see and imitate/mimic only our impressions of what we might perceive. Whether sketchy and vague, bewitching, or bright and powerful, our minds create artistic impressions and expressions that are often interwoven with our natural instincts and intuitions.

Whether in mundane life or any other field of our various activities, we still have no clear awareness of ourselves as spectators present in everything we perceive. Heisenberg's extraordinary discovery of the unavoidable effect stemming from the unavoidable presence of the observer must be mentioned here: in our mundane life, sciences or elsewhere, this finding has ended the fairytale of objectivity in our observations and perceptions of all types. However, curiously, most of the scientific beliefs that we come across, learn about, or analyze have a "reality of absolute truth" that remains commonly acceptable.

Regrettably many of us remain poorly superficial observers.

Curiously, the behaviors of abnormality seen in conditions such as "identity disorder" or "split personality," described in the field of psychology, are actually naturally present in all of us in different degrees of intensity. What we do with this ability is our circumstantial choice.

The more we learn from our own mind's behavior, the better and more beneficial we understand *how* our stories can be played in the minds that we observe and interact with. The more varieties of characters we play in our thinking (not forgetting about our own characters of selves), the wealthier our knowledge becomes. Everything is based on our continuous *comparisons* among characters empowered by our internal "mechanism of perceptions." One needs to become a great talent or theatrical genius such as Shakespeare to develop and animate so many meaningful and interactive characters in action on stage, and never suffering from a "split personality disorder."

The great artistic mind of Shakespeare created all of these characters by acting them out, all by itself, repeatedly at first in the imaginative theater of his single mind; however, the role of an observer who dominates all scenarios is the mind of the master artist. In this way, every mind senses it's self, especially as a leading character, even while mimicking others.

We perceive by imitating, similar to our conscious understanding, characters to follow, critique, deny, and even curse.

The majority of us are unaware of the inborn freedom of the little creators we are and here just to *be*, granted to us by God's nature. However, some of us are taking this very blessed responsibility for life as we are to perform it and learn in endlessly unique ways our freedom to choose the best possible roles for ourselves. Instinctively or intentionally, we learn who we are and where we want to be, often despite the most convoluted man-made social structure in which we might be trapped. Every living being aims to find harmonies of goodness and safety while instinctively feeling gratitude to Mother Nature who nourishes us all.

Our intuitive talents may reveal themselves to us in different forms, like musicians performing a classical musical composition gracefully and beautifully, and perfectly in tune with a leading composition. Conversely, unintuitive individuals like those untalented in music can make a lovely musical piece sound unrecognizably disturbing and alarming. Several disorders can also affect our inborn acting ability. Dissociative identity disorder (DID), previously called multiple personality disorder and commonly referred to as split personality or dissociative personality disorder, causes different personality conditions, and the disorder vary. DID usually results from excessive and unendurable stress or trauma, which commonly occurs during childhood. Recognition of a unified identity develops from a variety of experiences and sources. People can be susceptible to identity disorders when, during their childhood, they have been overwhelmed or traumatized by certain life experiences such as abuse, including repetitive negative experiences and even being subject to unstoppable positive and annoying "encouraging" control, humiliation, or violence. Every child who can walk and talk needs time for sovereign privacy to feel and form their unique character–that of the self. Although every child needs basic safeguarding, it is important to note that while supervision is necessary, it should not be invasive. The majority of adults have to keep in mind that small and cute children are not toys to be played with as part of games or adult fantasies.

As children are mainly talented imitators of what they observe, they try to understand "things" and living beings based on how they look and behave towards their own young selves. Intense control under superficial ignorance can greatly damage over time a growing, undeveloped character. Adaptation to repeatable habits of horrid behavior often destroys a young person before he or she grows onto an independent Self.

Poor education is commonly abusive as it treats children as empty jars. Starting from training individualities of very young students to "identify" themselves by glued to them given names, age, and address, this is already blocking the unique self-recognition naturally inborn in children. Explain before training that what you "teach" is important not to understand the world but to adjust one's existence in human society, the community, and the artificial rules to communicate therein, for the sake of survival in these conditions. While adapting to our artificially established society, we must learn on our own, as our own characters and abilities. Only our very powerful sense of inborn self-identity can help us separate manmade IDs, rules, laws, and training from the powers of our internal nature's existence.

A mind is born as a primordial actor, artist, director, and animator of its own unique experiences, turning these experiences into its own special action.

The mind is the primary art, sound recording, and animation studio, all of which take place in its own internal "chamber." Further, this little creator, one's mind, is composing and recomposing its character of self, as well as acting as its own observer of other characters while developing its own.

However, the sense of false "objectivity" prevails in primitive acting and thinking.

In parallel, we try to understand others by pretending to be the ones we observe and wish to understand; however, we shall never forget that our methods of understanding are mainly limited by the unintentional *mimicking* of others while we are thinking and staging our thoughts. We also describe and judge our impressions of others based on our own commonly primitive vision of these characters. Unavoidably, while describing others, we reveal our own internal acting abilities, whether they are very poor, average, brilliant, or thoughtful.

We must eventually admit that the internal forces of the mind, which we feel are driven by deep *intuition*, actually cannot be described in neither common nor scientific terms. This is an internal *natural mental compass*. With this internal *compass* guiding us, we may more intuitively sense and mimic others and more closely understand them as living beings.

We may see how a primitively thinking leader who is trying to use his "authorized" power to rule and control people sees living people as categorized and labeled in primitive groups of "identical" and "must-be-equal" units. As an unavoidable result, that leader's ignorance only provokes unthinkable resistance leading toward man-made disasters.

No matter what we may observe not only humans but every single living mind possesses two kinds of basic, deeply primordial *acting abilities,* which are as follows:

Mimicking talent is our inborn instinctive talent to develop our skills for adapting our behavior, mannerisms, and habits, which we first use to mimic adults when learning to make the sounds of their language to communicate with us and others. These mimicking abilities assist our basic survival in our man-made social environment. We acquire these skills through _imitation_ of what we see and hear, and we begin to develop these abilities from the moment we are born. Using these skills, we try to repeat, recreate, and even change or correct previously troubling behavioral and thinking habits.

This ability prevails during early childhood. It is essential not to expose a child to the extremities of society, as children might mimic horrific habits "for fun" without any sense of comprehension of what they are mimicking. These questionable childhood behaviors may lead to highly troubled circumstances in a child's future.

When we struggle as adults to learn a foreign language, we might feel surprised to see how easily small children begin to speak the same language; moreover, they mimic movements and mannerisms and behave like the children and adults around them, acting as their small reproductions.

After adapting to our social groups, we lose this talent while growing up. In most cases, we cannot change our old habits, accents, or mannerisms later in life. All that is stored in us similarly to canned food.

Creative talent is more uncommon, but is also inborn. This is the case with us at different levels, for we all have this ability. Breaking habits, behaviors, rules, and concepts and developing or creating new practical ideas and combinations of them often produces unpredictable results as we grow above our "old" selves. However, if we go about breaking anything without any new creative talent or skills _to replace the broken experience, rules, productions, and systems with a much greater alternative_, this does not stem from creative talent. Breaking the existing "things" just for the sake of it only indicates our weakness of mind, absence of intelligence, but great hostility, allowing perhaps ill but unrecognized psychological conditions to drive us toward big problems within and without that require serious remediation.

Major breakthroughs, inventions, and discoveries occur only due to creative talent.

The blessed combination of our acting, mimicking, and creative talents brings brilliant results to our knowledge and lives.

Consider the example of the Salk vaccine for polio. A field trial to test the vaccine was the most extensive effort of its kind that had ever occurred. Twenty thousand doctors and public health officers collaborated with 64,000 school staff and 220,000 volunteers, and more than 1.8 million school-age children participated. Before the introduction of a vaccine in 1955, polio was one of the most critical health threats worldwide, causing devastating outbreaks in the U.S. According to the Harvard School of Public Health, the 1952 U.S. outbreak, in which 3,145 people died and 21,269 were left with some form of paralysis, was the worst polio outbreak in the nation's history, and most of the victims were children. According to the 2009 PBS documentary _The Polio Crusade_, "Apart from the atomic bomb, America's greatest fear was polio."

The success of the vaccine trial was a truly lifesaving outcome. On April 12, 1955, the news went public, bringing accolades for Salk's outstanding work. Wide-scale vaccination efforts began swiftly, and Salk sought no profit from the vaccine, opting not to patent it so as to optimize its reach worldwide. Canada, the Netherlands, Sweden, and several other countries launched immunization efforts. In less than 25 years, the transmission of polio within the United States was completely eliminated and Salk was revered as a miracle worker.

This is a case revealing the presence of a great internal acting ability of a researcher's mind. Reflecting on his development of the vaccine, Salk offered these remarkable thoughts: "When I became a scientist, I would picture myself as a virus, or as a cancer cell, for example, and try to sense what it would be like to be either. I would also imagine myself as the immune system, and I would try to reconstruct what I would do as an immune system engaged in combating a virus or cancer cell. When I had played through a series of such scenarios on a particular problem and had acquired new insights, I would design laboratory experiments accordingly. I soon found myself in a dialogue with nature using viruses, immune systems, and other phenomena to ask questions in the form of experiments and then waiting for the answer. Based upon the results of the experiment, I would then know what questions to ask next, until I learned what I wanted to know, or until I went as far as I could go" (7). From the book *Anatomy of Reality: Merging Intuition and Reason* by Jonas Salk

As these words show, the superbly intuitive mind of this great researcher was empowered by his intuitive intellect, directing his perceptions of his reality—he almost "knows" where to look when embarking on the process of discovery. We still typically miss these intuitive perceptions of a great mind, which are left unnoticed by most trained professionals in the same field.

As we easily judge others, whether they are human beings that we cannot understand or animals whose intimate connection with nature is too complicated for us to truly fathom as a whole, we have endless learning ahead of us on how we can evolve our still-primitive theatrical mimicking of the realities of characters who are neither true idols to be admired nor stupid and primitive poppets.

However, there are no recipes for creating classical masterpieces in music, art, poetry, or philosophy. No AI can truly create on its own and remain as somewhat predictably functional models provided by the people who built it. Human intelligence, whether inborn or artificial, is still at the dawn of its development, far below the instinctive intelligence of any form of life that we may pretend to truly know. Thus, our man-made creations desperately need profound revisions at every possible level.

Our human character is diverse, as each of us play many different characters to understand others' actions, behaviors, and thinking. We are imitators of anyone and anything we observe, and not surprisingly, perhaps the most confused of all living beings we may observe.

Years ago, despite my poor circumstances, I was able to sculpt small figures, wondering if my unusual improvising artist's style could be possible in my sculpting work. The process of sculpting may turn into a very physically intense experience. Some gifted artists might at some point vividly feel that they breathe life into what they are composing in their hands.

I decided to sculpt the piece of clay as a totally blind artist, trusting only the sensations of touch. I never looked at my work during my work or afterward. I covered it with a light dark piece of fabric and suggested to the visitors that they only "see" my work using their hands, under the sculpture's covers. For me, the positive excitement of visitors was overwhelming. This was my most provocative artwork inviting my viewers to the unknown field revealing our instinctive perceptions.

We cannot imitate life of any sort but only mimic the characters we observe as grotesque caricatures mocking the living design of Mother Nature. Is our ability of producing our children related to our naturally creative process of continuity of life?

However, curiously, without understanding nature's vivid and magnificent ways, we insist on producing and using our very crude, and odd, primitive or complicated, models or machines.

What is the difference between nature's design within living wonders, and our artificial models of all sorts? If our art expressions can deliver highly emotional messages what are our man-made AI devices or systems doing for us? Why is that the man-made models are so disoriented in different environments as they have only a "frozen focus on what they are programmed to do?" Why are ultimately clumsy, unable to be intelligent on its own in ever-changing circumstances. If we are able to put aside our admiration and pride in ourselves, our man-made gadgets will look like grotesque caricatures when compared with living, reproductive, and self-adjustable natural creations. Man-made models of all types are unable to naturally adjust to the unpredictable environments within metamorphoses of Flux. In the first place, machines are not even handicapped, they are missing a life of their own.

Perhaps we can find some intriguing wisdom in Buddha's belief in the reincarnation of spirits and the endlessness of the journeys in living within different forms of bodies. Minds are spirits who are able to learn to evolve or devolve and are able to gain great experience while living and feeling as very many different forms of life.

While growing up, we are trained to identify and express ourselves to others from our artificially given generic names to IDs. Later, we express ourselves not only based on our generic names, but also by using our outfits and social positions, just as supportive insignificant actors on stages of our communities. One's identity is unique and given by nature at birth; however, it becomes suppressed and vaguely sensed by us, but remains deep in our minds, as every one of us is a unique living Self.

As we grow up, our mind is gradually blocked from the presence of the inborn creative Self by poor "education," manipulative knowledge, and mindless training intended to turn us into a complacent servant of established communities and institutions.

This is not about helping us develop our natural abilities or talents, but about training us to behave as a unit controlled by any type of incapable authority.

Our impressions of what we think we know are commonly questionable. Imagine a man visiting his future boss at his office, whom he has never met. The man enters the office and looks at the room where he is meeting his future boss. After the meeting, when he leaves the office, he feels sure he knows his future boss. However, in his memory, he can only recollect the boss's tone of voice and random positive words regarding his future work, along with part of his boss's face—some part of his mouth, nose, and shiny glasses perched on it—the vague color of his suit jacket, heaps of paper on the boss's desk, and just a part of the window filtering light behind the boss's head. The man's sketchy impression of his future boss is ultimately vague, and if we could depict it, it would look like a surrealistic and unfinished art piece. However, this is how the man "knows" his boss in his memory.

As such, what is our knowledge?

Perhaps it is our ability to memorize something and expect similar results from similar experiences in the future.

When we encounter something unexpected, we cannot know it because we have no previous experience.

"The creation of something new is not accomplished by the intellect but by the play instinct acting from inner necessity. The creative mind plays with the objects it loves," stated the greatest analyst of a human psyche within our contemporary society, Carl Jung.

Popular performances are monotonous on purpose—not to lose the attention of the mass audience, but to make spectators easily recognize the familiar moves, characters, sounds, looks etc., to satisfy a public that expects all that to watch and hear.

If you are a truly, naturally original and unusual poet or artist, you stand alone in your internal world by yourself, commonly unrecognized. Rarely does a great philosopher receive high praise while still alive, as it takes abundant time to gain appreciation, except by some rare chance or outstanding stroke of luck. Do not expect to be recognized by mass culture if you are new and authentically original. You stand alone, lonely and misunderstood, unrecognized by a society of people with shallow, randomly patched imagination, while the screaming vulgarities of fashion receive praise and idolization because, though insignificant, they are easy to notice on the surface.

Human mentality commonly relies on a very tricky pretentiousness—a propensity to act as someone or something that we are not! Although we imitate what we perceive in our thinking, fantasizing, and decision-making, many of us internally are not great actors when we must think on our own without guidance.

Everyone growing up in our society is trained to be polite, which means saying nice things even when feeling angry with others, to avoid upsetting them. Is politeness our first training in how to lie? What formal education is doing through such lessons warrants hundreds of books on what ethics truly mean to us?

A mind's acting abilities, whether poor, amusing, or impressive, are abilities for life.

Spinoza offered these words:

Whenever, then, anything in nature seems to us ridiculous, absurd, or evil, it is because we have but a partial knowledge of things, and in the main are ignorant of the order and coherence of nature as a whole, and because we want everything to be arranged according to the dictate of our own reason; although, in fact, what our reason pronounces bad, is not bad as regards the order and laws of universal nature, but only as regards the laws of our own nature taken separately. From *Ethics*, in *The Ethics Of Spinoza: The Road to Inner Freedom* by Benedict de Spinoza

He also asserts,

> Bad and good are prejudices which the eternal reality cannot recognize … And as with good and bad, so with the ugly and the beautiful; these too are subjective and personal terms which, flung at the universe, will be returned to the sender unhonored. "I would warn you that I do not attribute to nature either beauty or deformity, order or confusion. Only in relation to our imagination can things be called beautiful or ugly, well-ordered or confused."

> Based on the remarkable acting abilities we develop in life, we gradually become our own parents while looking after ourselves. This characterizes what we recognize as adulthood. In this way, we can grow up along with our children. Our acting talents are never fixed and are energized by our self-produced emotional pulsations.

CHAPTER FIVE

Emotional Flow and Circulation of Instant Sensations of Energy, Igniting Vitality

We feel sensations in every moment; however, whether awake, asleep, unwell, in pain, feeling joy, or feeling balanced, we cannot see, calculate, or photograph what we sense in these moments. We are "made of" these ever-new instances, of sensations flowing as Heraclitus' River of life, the living energies throughout our very existence. Life is metamorphic, whether we feel our experience as "physical" or "mental." Each unique form of life prolongs its existence by self-producing internal energy. Sensations are forever emerging and melting, and forever more or less new. They create rivers of feelings, whether powerful or "slow" or insignificant; they run throughout the mind, and whether positively or negatively, strikingly affect the bodily heart, vitalizing the rest of a living body. Instances of living sensations are deeply intuitive sparks or signals that come from our perception of ever-changing environments, whether we feel them consciously or not.

There is a grand difference between sensations stemming from the world of living beings and those that are man-manufactured, technologically transmitted pixels. The latter appears to us sighted human beings as one-dimensional images collected on flat screens of computers or gadget displays.

Artificially produced signals may mimic our living sensations but do not use what we may recognize as living emotional energy. Artificial pixels require artificial energy to energize them and be transmitted. All technologies are dead from the moment they are made.

In contrast to the naturally fluctuating instances of sensation with which our self-productions of living energies ignite our minds, all contemporary technologies unintentionally mimic our mental perception process and collect not living sensations but pixel-like dead signals artificially transmitted onto flat surfaces, screens, and prints in an effort to copy the mind's unreal illusions, demonstrating a similar effect to our experience of composing visions in our minds. These artificial methods only confuse and often overwhelm our superficial theatrical imagination of the mind as we create on the flat stages of what we identify as consciousness. The ghosts built by pixels are not living beings.

Unlike humans, animals and other living beings are not easily confused when perceiving visual effects based on artificially flattened images. Animals typically sense the flat surfaces of these illusions.

Perhaps when we live in mostly artificial environment of our everyday life we become suffocated and desperate for the truly living and breathing environments in open nature, exchanging with us fulfilling vital highly emotional living energies.

We are excitable creatures commonly living in our internal scenarios of life, unaware that our scenarios in the theatrical consciousness of our minds can be drastically different from the actual conditions of our outer environment. The naturally emotional excitement creates the same effect in our minds as ocean waves create for a ship. Our minds could enjoy the tranquility of peacefully drifting or a spirited wind that speeds us up and takes us far away, or we could experience the horror of a powerful storm sending our minds to the bottom of the ocean of our emotions. The power of our emotions can cure or destroy our bodies and perhaps our minds.

Unlike any manmade robotic device that requires artificial energy to run, our living minds always self-produce unique energies within ourselves from ever-new instances of sensations.

It is no wonder that many people feel somewhere deep inside that they are spirits, souls, or ephemeral entities unfamiliar with physics, chemistry, or biology. In addition, our bodies certainly need energy from food and water to exist as living compositions. Artificially produced food eventually starves and kills living bodies because of the absence of living energy, which is invisible to the sciences and ignorant consumers.

In our world, true repetitions, perfect balance, symmetry, equality, identical events or units like numbers, and our imaginative laws such as the law of conservation of energy are impossible. We can only fantasize about these perfect conditions based on our very crude measurements and calculus.

Before we can feel any type of physical need, such as hunger when our physical body needs food or some rest, we must have *the ability to produce some primary feelings.*

We feel or sense the power, which is unnamed and uncaptured by any device, all the time, consciously and subconsciously, running through our mind and body, while we are awake or asleep, even in a coma, when our bodily functions are supported by artificial medical methods and devices. Some of us call this energy spiritual, some call it emotional, and some consider it supernatural. However, in any case, this very power remains mysterious to us, as it clearly has ephemeral control over our physical senses, blood circulation, and nervous system from the moment of bodily birth to the moment of death. It stays unknown to us because it is physically immeasurable and invisible. I would not dare coin any pretentious-sounding scientific name for it; instead, I wish to use a plain term for the sake of convenience in writing further about it. I call it *primordial living energy*, recognizing it as the energy that gives us our primarily sensual and sensitive abilities to uniquely perceive and feel our bodily experience of the specific material world of gravity where our temporary body lives. We exchange this *primordial* energy with all other living beings. It is the energy of our circulating within ourselves *emotions.*

Without the ability to produce sensations within our minds, we would be unable to feel our bodies at all. We cannot feel hunger, pain, or joy, and like any other life form, we cannot stay alive in any reality of the world if our invisible senses are "unplugged" for any possible reason.

When, as a small child, I fell on the ground from a garden bench because I had jumped on it very carelessly to see if I could fly, I concluded that God gave us pain not to make us suffer, but to prevent us from engaging in quick acts of self-destruction; thus, we could understand pain as a warning signal for danger.

Pain means that we are limited. Later, I was introduced to several different opinions explaining our senses and feelings, all random attempts to make very minor progress in our logical ability to understand them. Perhaps we do not take our emotions as seriously as our physical or bodily experiences, because we mistakenly associate our senses with our physical status as the root reason. We multiply our mistakes because we pay no attention to the fact that our physical existence is impossible without our emotional energy. It might sound strange to some, but I am not referring to emotions as the product of physical processes; rather, I mean that this very energy from sensations is produced in our minds.

Our mind's *pre-emotional* status has potential control over our physical body, giving life to our bodily functions.

Life of any nature is all about its unique interactions, which, when integrated, become a great driving source for every life form.

A living mind is impossible to unplug.

CHAPTER SIX

The Geography of the Living Creative Mind

In my rendering below, I depict the composition of a living human mind that presumably fits within its own ephemeral sphere, internally possessing interconnected layers.

These layers may develop or decline uncountably; however, I present only three easily recognizable mental layers on which I suggest focusing.

I shaped my rendering as a sphere, which might remind the viewer of the traditional spherical presentations of the heavens and cosmic figures throughout history. However, my presentation demonstrates a drastically opposite meaning to all preceding renderings. My drawing is not that of the traditional composition of the universe, heavens with celestial bodies, or the cosmos, as the authors of these presentations imagine that these subjects show us as existing above and around us. The sphere that we are looking at in my drawing is an image of the composition of an interactive, living human mind that we observe within ourselves.

A HUMAN MIND HAS 3 BASIC
INTERACTIVE SPHERES ONE
INSIDE THE OTHER

First - SUBCONSCIOUS
Second - COSMIC
Third - PHYSICAL

Neither Cosmic nor Physical realities can exist without Subconscious part of a mind.

CONTEMPLATION 1 on "Geography of Living Mind" by V. Nova

Scholars' and philosophers' historical and traditional depictions show the imaginative mighty world shaped as circles or spheres and furnish them with what we see as cosmic landscapes with the sun, moon, earth, and other celestial bodies, with their presumable relations in symbols, numbers, or locations, while showing their imaginative characters and figures.

The popular images of the scholarly sphere that appear to our sight are above our bodily heads in the skies. These descriptions and explanations miss the very presence of the **perceiver**, observer, author, and creator of the appearances visible to them. We observe and render these visions, imitating our mental ephemeral production, which has *already been processed previously within our mental mechanism of perceptions*. This means that in traditional spherical pictures, we see expressions, not of objective events outside us, but of internal mental events affected by our ephemeral interactions with the environments of Flux, including the appearances of what we may intensely sense as our physical bodies. Our mental sensations are the very materials we may experience and express.

As the internal observers of our mind's production, we may perceive all that only within each of our minds, never without, no matter what kinds of metamorphoses and transformations there might be of the worlds we might interact with.

Because our minds are creators and self-observers from within, we cannot jump outside ourselves to see the world as it is for the sake of the safety of our unique life.

I begin my notes by describing the nature of its existence as metamorphic as it can be: There are no stars out there, no trees or water.

We can explore, observe, feel, act, and create only when we reside within our minds.

For the first time, I invite the curious to follow the process of our perception while observing the ephemeral geography of the mind.

I suggest identifying the first vital layer of mind as the *SUPERCONSCIOUSNESS*, rather than what we vaguely recognize as "subconsciousness." The layer of *SUPERSUBCONSCIOUS* of mind is where a human being receives the most primary, immediate, yet random interactions with the outer environment of mighty nature.

That is where we might find how to sense and feel the most primary and powerful interactions, perceiving instant effects from the endless transformations of the Flux.

It is also the layer of mind where its limitations begin to create powerful *protective boundaries* to shield the internal ephemeral formation of a living mind from exposure to harmful effects coming from the colossal turns of *Flux* outside. These are moments at the beginning of our unique creative work of our life, shaping and reshaping our internal realities.

Flux is the endless vital source of the energies igniting all of our abilities and talents to create and recreate ourselves from its inexhaustible powers.

The SUPERCONSCIOUSNESS "First" layer, is where we may sense this deeply intuitive vitality energizing our minds as something our bodily sensations vaguely perceive.

For astonishing reasons that await our discovery, *SUPERCONSCIOUSNESS* may produce a translucently acute perception within a powerfully lucid reality that our bodily sensations are unable to reach.

We shall begin discovering this field of our *SUPERCONSCIOUSNESS* presently, in particular in, *the after-death experience,* as the recent growing numbers of records show the possibilities of our reaching realities unknown to physical sensation, and which are the most outstanding of all experiences we may have in our memories as living human beings.

With the indirect help of improved medical technology, which was impossible in the past, medical doctors have conducted new procedures to resuscitate clinically dead patients under their care. The collected records have been based on all possible post-mortem tests before resuscitation.

The revival of these dead bodies has enabled many to share what we recognize at the present time to be life *after bodily death* in a clinical setting. The patients who have survived clinical death report the astonishing results of a mental existence, not only feeling and sensing without bodily organs but also proving the mind entity to be a powerful and extremely vigorous presence. Unlike dreams or hallucinations, the after-death experience reveals things unknown to the patient, who, once he loses all bodily functions and sensations, gains sudden clarity and strikingly lucid vision, and the mind's will without possessing physical eyes, ears, or bodies to move or using words to communicate.

A recent pioneering research directly related to resuscitation **studies** was written and published in *Consciousness Beyond Life* by Pim van Lomell, a world-renowned cardiologist. This richly informative book is a must-read for all who can find it. These after-death experiences are never the same and present a great challenge for researchers to analyze afterdeath experiences expressed in our limited conventional language. I have had my own experience such as this, and I must state that no words can describe even remotely what I have experienced, except for one extraordinary point upon which all those revived from clinical death agree—the striking lucidity and penetrating clarity of perceptions of reality and one's bodiless entity in it, and the instant ease of telepathic comprehension of one's endlessly deep surrounds—all that makes physical heavy physical reality that often excites us—a strange, hopelessly insignificant dream one does not want to "re-visit."

The SECOND Layer is the COSMIC Layer, which is "located" next to the *SUPERCONSCIOUSNESS.*

This is where cosmic appearances become visible to us and where we may observe through our corporeal or physical organs, especially sight. We sense and observe picturesque and theatrically playful landscapes of "consciousness" staged by our mind. These visions of things distant from our bodies, the starry universe or cosmos, are built through our temporary sensations sifted by our perceptions through our limited bodily organs. *The Second or COSMIC Layer* of the mind is a temporary event that may disappear after the mind disconnects from its interactions with its corporeal body.

The Third *CONSCIOUSNESS Layer is a* burlesque *pictorial* theater of the mind that emerges from the Second *COSMIC layer.* It is where we feel corporeal "touchable" reality.

The temporary existence of what we recognize as *CONSCIOUSNESS* is the result of sensations multiply digested and overly sifted in our minds, bringing experiences of crucial pain or joy while depriving this physical experience of the most deeply vital, primary sensations from the *SUPERCONSCIOUS* layer of the mind.

The layer of *CONSCIOUSNESS* is not only very superficial and temporary, but also crudely blocks our bodily experience from our primary and highly vital and deeply intuitive experience within *SUPERCOUNSCIOUSNESS.*

As human beings, we are extremely excited to explore temporary bodily sensations of presumably controllable tangible bodies. This temporary reality is possible when we see, hear, touch, and feel, when our minds stage these sensations while using our corporeal eyes, ears, brains, and other bodily organs.

The superficial theatrical stages of this layer of CONSCIOUSNESS are events in which we are temporarily involved as vigorous players trying to control our scenarios of physical reality; however, we mistakenly recognize and identify ourselves as only our visible bodily characters and appearances. Though these bodily appearances change tremendously on their own, whether bringing pain or comfort and even excitement, as our mental interactions with bodies continue across time by temporarily transforming our environments; while we are playing our physically imbodied personalities of "selves," we curiously trust that these bodies are truly our authentic Selves. The conflicts between bodily appearances and minds are inevitable.

Our temporary physical bodies are never solid formations but highly complicated coexistences of diverse, ever-transforming living organisms, which we mistakenly see as solid bodies.

All three depicted layers are the sovereign residence of the unique spirit of a living being. Extremely vivid in all its functions, the *sphere* of each human mind is a wonderland of its Sovereign Self. Many of us deeply sense this very Self as a spirit, soul, or a living entity of some sort.

While all our primary sensations are possible through the natural *mechanism of perceptions*, our living mind remains its own spectator and interpreter of its wondrous existence, embracing, composing, and re-composing what it may sense while continuously perceiving its ever-changing environments. The powers of interactive sensations of each living mind are the marvelous work creating our own internal and unique productions, and these are our own endlessly transforming mental universes.

A mind is a creator, its own unique spectator and observer.

The natural worlds are invisible unless perceived within living minds, yet our unseen and unsensed realities wait for us within timeless mental journeys into the endlessness of Flux.

If one prefers to understand one's reality by "simplifying" the task—seeking to base one's life on the temporary and greatly fluctuating bodily visions appearing in one's superficial consciousness, or the picturesque ones in the *Cosmic layer* — these visions can only provide questionable proof of our true reality, as this is based on what one's corporeal eyes "reflect." In these cases, the world appears to be as primitive as one's simplified, superficial puzzle of pictures missing endless pieces, and one would uselessly search for flattish staged appearances to complete the forever incomplete puzzle of random, awkwardly misaligned fragments. Nature's powers within the existence of everything in it are not held in such primitive modeling.

The great practitioner, when designing and building his building, knows well that it is never complete and would need constant maintenance even after his great building stands fully functional.

From the perspective of the physical body, scholars have continuously sought to explain the visions and beliefs of the fantastic cosmic landscapes perceived through human sight, as if they were objective outsiders. They never could. We are not "very small beings" as some nearsighted astronomer might express the admiration of cosmic impressions through human corporeal sight. The creations of cosmos with our tiny bodies in it is produced and staged in a mind of the observer.

Most curiously, many of us do not bother to find out that our perceptions and interpretations of "the world" have been entirely digested within our own thinking minds. Amazingly, to this very day, the contemporary sciences use super telescopes and satellites to produce impressive photos and videos of cosmic landscapes, and their practitioners still believe in just the same illusive notion that they are exploring the "outer world" by reflecting it.

CONTEMPLATION 2 on "Geography of Living Mind" by V. Nova

A mind, the sovereign sphere of its highly interactive existence, is never closed or solid. No one can watch or spy on any living mind but its own.

Our minds are little creators, as we are blessed by our abilities with unique living tools to compose and recompose our realities granted to us from birth by God's nature for life.

The mighty world out there is something we can never sense directly and do not need to, as it is incomprehensible in the myriad of its existences.

As we all go through a unique experience living as human bodies on Earth, we often feel bewildered about what all this may be and why we struggle and fight so hard, yet our bodies still die.

Thus, I suggest conceptualizing the composition of a temporary body with which we interact through our responsibilities, as we are able to comprehend the mental digestive process within the "stomach" in the deep "center" of our mind, as shown above. The reality of a physical experience is hardly digestible by the human mind and is eventually as easily disposable as any digestive process.

Our minds learn to be temporary guardians of our bodies, while our bodies affect our mental sensations and feelings, bringing unique experiences to our ephemeral existence. Revisions of what we do and think are thus greatly overdue.

People commonly paint their faces and bodies with makeup to beautify skin that they consider unattractive or undergo plastic surgeries to trim and "shape up" their bodies according to societal standards of beauty. What do we miss in our ways of living? Does a graceful horse or swan need plastic surgery, or a gorgeous hummingbird technology and a ton of fuel to fly back and forth as it pleases, or a mountain goat special artificial parts for its legs, along with clothing, food, water, and heavy equipment, to climb to breathtaking heights? Animal leaders take their families to safety and sources of food and water, whereas human leaders take ignorant human crowds to endless disasters and destruction.

What should we learn from being intimately involved with vulnerable human bodies while discovering the most vital abilities of our sovereign minds?

To discover the nature of the mind itself, we have to visit a mind's living "domain" behind what we observe as pictorial landscapes, oceans, trees, movements and formations of all sorts, things and matter, molecules, genes or bacteria, our memories and dreams, beyond everything we see using our "naked eye" even when they are augmented through super microscopes or telescopes.

We would not need any technology, such as super microscopes or telescopes, because these tools have been built after our human physical sense-perception, mainly corporeal sight. For a change, let us admit that the corporeal sight we use for all mundane and scientific observations and practices has proven to be the most unreliable, illusive, and deceiving of all the physical sense perceptions that we humans may possess.

EPILOGUE

The Great Revision of Our Highly Questionable Experience with Nature and Ourselves in It

Erwin Schrödinger in his *Mind and Matter* explains that man's picture of the world is a construct of his own mind. This deeply intuitive thought needs to be explained.

Is distance real? How do we follow Newtonian and Einsteinian laws to survive as living bodies within the colossal powers of Flux?

Is the speed of light only the ultimate speed of our human perception of physical sight, not of the world? Can we extrapolate different speeds of a universal nature as speeds of change to enable us to at least crudely conceptualize events beyond our limited corporeal perception of sight?

Mentioning Galileo, Newton, and Laplace, who imaginatively explained the world, will we one day be able to add to this fabulous list the name of a blind-from-birth great scientist?

How do we sense resistance while believing that we touch something "material"?

If we think of the genetic level when describing the living structure of cells, are our children's genes older than ours, and are our children genetically older than their parents who produce their bodies?

All the answers lie deeply inside our own selves.

Most revolutionary discoveries in history have been rooted in the deep inner intuition within the minds of great men.

The worlds of universal nature ignited by the powers of Flux are invisible in their instants. We are entirely interactive, but may never reflect upon and observe anything outside ourselves. From minuscule viruses to colossal cosmic formations, all that we might observe is the result of the wondrous production of each of our human minds, composing our primary instant sensations from transformations of Flux. A mind is able to see only through the living mechanism of its inborn mental perceptions.

The most effective means to evolve ourselves is to start learning from within while collecting the most honest experiences of others. To find intelligent and exciting coexistence together is to learn that we are not one identical entity but many diverse living beings.

Each of our minds is the observer of the Self. If we only observe the stages of our curious theatrical *consciousness*—illusive and wobbly—no one would succeed in attaining intelligent self-awareness.

Our blessed inborn creativity is highly abused in our closed man-made societies of fictions of fixed ideas-for-all, and our transparent tricks, pretenses, and disguises just to control, and take as much as possible from others, including physical destructions. We are deadly *abusive toward Creativity for life*. Therefore, we go nowhere from a state of primitive blindness and poor, angry, hectic, hurting, and hating human selves. It is about human great arrogance rising high from the bitter helplessness of not knowing.

The world's wisdom is endlessly vital and astonishingly inviting to live in its nature while getting to know it.

No real balance, exact equality, equity, identical copies of anything, repetitions, symmetry, conservation of energy, perfect reversal, or absolute isolation is ever possible under the colossal power of *Flux*.

Centuries ago, pioneering scholars had to take responsibility for inventing their own ways of research and discovery, had to invent and build equipment for themselves, and proceeded to test what they sought to discover, independently of the ruling forces or social systems of their time.

However, these days, scientists are hired and well-paid to uphold ideas and explanations controlled by governments' rules aligned with corporate or political interests.

Have we been mistaken in explaining our many questionable activities as great achievements and intelligence, especially in the sciences and technology, where professionals, scholars, and researchers are hired and paid to "create" proof of ideas made up to serve authorities, ignorant idealists, or industrial or political rulers?

We often hear great excitement over media soundbites, with little or no learning behind the locked doors of the contemporary scholarly labs and institutions producing such manipulated "achievements."

If in the near future basic education would provide basic new learning from students' childhood—that no one can fly out of oneself to observe the world objectively and independently, as no one can skip the very process of unique perception of our minds and their interpretations—our society would be able to learn better ethics and awareness of living in our artificial societies, and even find wisdom in living nature where we are born.

The sciences, as we know them today, provide no true knowledge of ourselves or nature, the ultimate living teacher that we may know. Rather, we learn only by manipulating its design in our closed-off labs and wasting millions on hellish and useless research, including the capture and torture of millions of live animals. The great observer of human nature, Arthur Schopenhauer, asked such researchers, "How can you sleep at night?" (*Essays and Aphorisms* 1851).

We can look to some singularly horrific experiments done in the past, such as those of the monster-mind medical researcher Pavlov, who captured hungry homeless dogs for his hellish experiments to "professionally" demonstrate that dogs could be conditioned to salivate at the sound of a bell if that sound were repeatedly presented at the same time that they were shown food. Do you wonder why Pavlov needed to torture and starve dogs to death to come up with such trivial facts, rather than using himself?

However, truly pioneering achievements in history by researchers of genius provide superb examples of humane research motivated by the highest ethics. Examples of such pioneers include Louis Pasteur, the French chemist and microbiologist renowned for his principles of vaccination, and Jonas Salk, who created the *vaccine for polio*.

As we now live in the 21st century, the soberly rapid development of our conditions is the most crucial factor for our survival as human beings.

The most devastating practices abusing contemporary technologies while missing all the factual evidence and ethical criteria of true knowledge are serving the highly questionable ideas of "climate change." Highly cynical and ignorant groups of politically placed individuals who have installed themselves to manipulate and mess with our still poorly researched planetary conditions have already quietly come up with outrageously deadly global activities. Curiously, these activities are unauthorized by international public bodies and governments.

This global geoengineering activity refers to "fixing" the Earth's very thin atmosphere by daily spraying megatons of deadly particulates of heavy metals, chemicals, and plastic microparticles, which not only bring disasters to the Earth's atmosphere but are rapidly poisoning and killing all life forms on our planet, as this hellish man-produced pollution in the air we breathe is landing daily in the soil and water and easily penetrating through our lungs and brains.

The outstanding scientists and researchers who do not follow the orders of the rulers of society are tirelessly working on testing air, soil, water, and living forms of life, which are declining at a great speed. Dane Wigington, a brilliant, internationally recognized researcher entirely devoted to watching the sinister activities of geoengineering and reporting them on his site GeoengeneringWarch.org, states:

"Climate engineering may be the least worst climate solution," says a new report from CleanTechnica. After over 75 years of climate intervention operations, clearly, the CleanTechnica conclusion couldn't be further from the truth. A new U.N. report headline has just stated "science points to climate collapse," but the climate engineering component in the equation is, of course, never mentioned. A new Weather Channel report asks "Do Changing Temperatures Make You Sick?" Would it be more appropriate to ask if it's what is in the changing weather that's making us sick? For the record, cloud seeding fallout from climate engineering operations is contaminating our precipitation. This isn't speculation, it is a lab testing proven fact. And above it all the deterioration of the ozone layer continues to accelerate as new reports have just confirmed. How long till impact?

What is "DIMMING THE SUN?"

"A recent geoengineering patent promotes the spraying of highly toxic dimethylamine into our skies to enhance cloud formation….Toxic skies, toxic seas, toxic everything, how much longer can we survive on a dying planet? Is there still time to turn the tide? The latest installment of Global Alert News is below. All are needed in <u>the critical battle to wake populations</u> to what is coming, <u>we must make every day count</u>. Share <u>credible data</u> from a credible source, and make your voice heard."

<u>*Dane Wigington*</u>
<u>*GeoengineeringWatch.org*</u>

The grand responsibility for disasters of this sort lies with the governments and populations in a sleepwalking state.

The methods of any authentic research must be free from the control of typically ignorant and weak-minded authorities who only seek to enforce their highly questionable ideas and goals and, above all, benefit from their crooked manipulations.

We still have to somehow comprehend together that our structured society with its leading fictitious ideas is not the world, and the governments that we must select according to our knowledge and intelligence, are not to rule its citizens but *to serve* and protect them.

How much do we truly know about our nature just from the appearance of the universe?

Are we human beings ready to be "the masters of the universe" based on our contemporary intelligence?

Mimicking is a prevalent human character that commonly leads individuals and blindly excited crowds or mobs to catastrophes.

This means that, at the present time, if the global authorities have decided that the planet Earth is rotating-in-the-wrong-direction and must be stopped along with "dangerous climate change," the naïve majorities of the human population would start pouring donations into this new "life-saving project to stop the earth from rotation."

The main goal for our survival is to squirm out of the hellish ignorance of the globalists' grasp, and

stop reckless global activities that are highly poisonous in every way and everywhere. At this very moment these global activities are based on colossal human arrogance and ignorance, misleading the confused masses who are driving themselves into the abyss of madness. We must comprehend that *freedom without responsibilities equals madness.*

The magnificent school of nature is open to all of us, but our willingness to learn from it is blocked by our own human arrogance.

When our loud cacophonies are destroying us and we are screaming, losing our own singing voices, the blessed and deeply vital creative abilities we are granted will come to rescue us, leading us to safety and harmoniously meaningful survival.

The Human Exploration of Cosmos/Laundry Day

BY DISCOVERING THE NATURAL LAWS OF OUR REALITIES WE DISCOVER
THE LAWS OF OUR OWN PERCEPTION — NOT THE "OUTER" WORLD'S LAWS.
The existence that we all experience is possible because of the unique work of our
sensory perceptions forever governed by the internal laws of our minds. The laws
of the world out there are still unknown to us because of the tremendous limitations
in our perceiving. We have a new age of grand discoveries in front of us if we
accept the new basic structure of a mind peacefully embracing our ideas and expe-
reance in an entirely new, innovative order.

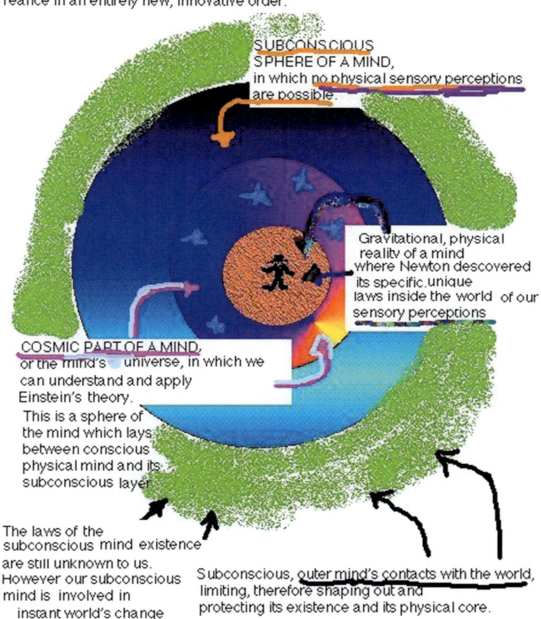

SUBCONSCIOUS
SPHERE OF A MIND,
in which no physical sensory perceptions
are possible.

Gravitational, physical
reality of a mind
where Newton descovered
its specific, unique
laws inside the world of our
sensory perceptions

COSMIC PART OF A MIND,
or the mind's universe, in which we
can understand and apply
Einstein's theory.

This is a sphere of
the mind which lays
between conscious
physical mind and its
subconscious layer.

The laws of the
subconscious mind existence
are still unknown to us.
However our subconscious
mind is involved in
instant world's change

Subconscious, outer mind's contacts with the world,
limiting, therefore shaping out and
protecting its existence and its physical core.

CONTEMPLATION 3 on "Geography of Living Mind" by V. Nova

"ABOUT TIME" by V. Nova

Clocks are churches to venerate Time.
They are built for minds bewitched by the illusion of its power.
Humans hurry their existence.
They know more about hours and minutes than about what they are,
facing new years as new worlds to count.
Time measures stars to fit them in the space of thoughts.
Clocks tick away the rest and labor, love and hatred,
horror and joy
the same way we calculate the same units in math.
People mark the same identical minutes in birth and death.

It was no time before I opened my eyes to see the world.
My heart started my clock and my time began.
My days are as long as I move.
Thoughts are years. Minutes of hate are shorter than seconds,
minutes of love and thanks longer than my existence.

I cannot be late for myself—I am always on time.
My mind is the only time machine,
which takes me everywhere, ignoring millions of years.
I could see my life as one day, but I need centuries to
understand a moment.
When my heart stops my time,
no one will be there to rewind it.

END?
No. The beginning of the great revision of what we know and exploring

"SOUNDLESS VIEW" original painting on canvas, 36" x 48" by Vera Nova

Printed in the United States
by Baker & Taylor Publisher Services